ENERGY POLICIES, POLITICS AND PRICES

FEDERAL ENERGY MANAGEMENT AND GOVERNMENT EFFICIENCY GOALS

ENERGY POLICIES, POLITICS AND PRICES

Additional books in this series can be found on the Nova website under the Series tab.

Additional E-books in this series can be found on the Nova website under the E-books tab.

ENERGY POLICIES, POLITICS AND PRICES

FEDERAL ENERGY MANAGEMENT AND GOVERNMENT EFFICIENCY GOALS

AMELIA R. WILLIAMS
EDITOR

Novinka
Nova Science Publishers, Inc.
New York

For permission to use material from this book please contact us:
Telephone 631-231-7269; Fax 631-231-8175
Web Site: http://www.novapublishers.com

LIBRARY OF CONGRESS CATALOGING-IN-PUBLICATION DATA
Available upon request

ISBN: 978-1-60692-985-8

Published by Nova Science Publishers, Inc. ✦ New York

CONTENTS

PREFACE

The federal government is the nation's single largest energy consumer, spending approximately $17 billion in fiscal year 2007 on energy for buildings and vehicles. This total represents almost 1 percent of all federal expenditures and these costs have been rising in recent years. In light of these energy price increases, congressional interest in making the federal government more energy efficient has grown as well. Although the federal fleet is less than 1 percent of all vehicles on the road in the U.S. today, Congress and the administration have established energy conservation objectives for the federal fleet in an effort to provide leadership in reducing petroleum consumption. This new book gathers the latest data from the Federal Energy Management office and explores current government energy efficiency goals.

Chapter 1 - Congress and the administration set forth energy objectives for federal fleets with 20 or more vehicles. Agencies are to (1) acquire alternative fuel vehicles (AFV) as 75 percent of all new light-duty vehicle acquisitions; (2) use only alternative fuel in AFVs, unless granted a waiver; (3) increase overall alternative fuel use by 10 percent annually;(4) reduce petroleum consumption by 2 percent annually through 2015; and (5) purchase plug-in hybrid electric vehicles when available and at a reasonable cost. The first two objectives are requirements in the Energy Policy Acts (EPAct) of 1992 and 2005. The last three are goals set by Executive Order 13423. GAO was asked to determine agencies' compliance with these objectives for fiscal year 2007 and how agencies are poised to meet them in the future. GAO obtained and analyzed information from the Department of Energy's (DOE) automotive database and other sources and interviewed agency officials.

Chapter 2 - The federal government is the nation's single largest energy consumer, spending approximately $17 billion in fiscal year 2007. A number of statutes and executive orders have established and revised goals directing agencies to reduce energy consumption and greenhouse gas emissions—such as carbon dioxide, which results from combustion of fossil fuels and natural processes, among other things—and increase renewable energy use. GAO was asked to determine the extent to which (1) federal agencies met energy efficiency, greenhouse gas emission, and renewable energy goals in fiscal year 2007; (2) federal agencies have made progress in each of these areas in the recent past; and (3) six selected agencies are poised to meet energy goals into the future. For this review, GAO, among other things, conducted site visits for six agencies and reviewed the Department of Energy's (DOE) annual reports to Congress on federal energy management.

In: Federal Energy Management and Government... ISBN: 978-1-60692-985-8
Editor: Amelia R. Williams

Chapter 1

FEDERAL ENERGY MANAGEMENT AGENCIES ARE ACQUIRING ALTERNATIVE FUEL VEHICLES BUT FACE CHALLENGES IN MEETING OTHER FLEET OBJECTIVES*

U.S. Government Accountability Office

WHY GAO DID THIS STUDY

Congress and the administration set forth energy objectives for federal fleets with 20 or more vehicles. Agencies are to (1) acquire alternative fuel vehicles (AFV) as 75 percent of all new light-duty vehicle acquisitions; (2) use only alternative fuel in AFVs, unless granted a waiver; (3) increase overall alternative fuel use by 10 percent annually;(4) reduce petroleum consumption by 2 percent annually through 2015; and (5) purchase plug-in hybrid electric vehicles when available and at a reasonable cost. The first two objectives are requirements in the Energy Policy Acts (EPAct) of 1992 and 2005. The last three are goals set by Executive Order 13423. GAO was asked to determine agencies' compliance with these objectives for fiscal year 2007 and how agencies are poised to meet them in the future. GAO obtained and analyzed

* This is an edited, reformatted and augmented version of a U. S. Government Accountability Office publication dated October 2008.

information from the Department of Energy's (DOE) automotive database and other sources and interviewed agency officials.

WHAT GAO RECOMMENDS

GAO recommends that DOE (1) report on agencies' compliance with the requirement to use alternative fuel in AFVs, (2) revise its guidance to disallow AFV credits for AFVs not subject to the acquisition requirement, and (3) continue to work with the General Services Administration to resolve data-quality issues. Congress should consider aligning the federal fleet AFV acquisition and fueling requirements with current alternative fuel availability and revising them as appropriate.

WHAT GAO FOUND

Federal agencies had mixed results in meeting the energy objectives for fleets in fiscal year 2007. First, all the agencies reported meeting or exceeding the requirement to acquire AFVs. However, they did so partly based on receiving credit for AFVs not subject to the requirement, as allowed by the DOE's implementing guidance. For example, AFVs outside large metropolitan areas do not count when agencies establish their acquisition targets, but they do count toward meeting the targets. Second—regarding the requirement to use only alternative fuel in AFVs—neither DOE nor the agencies reported on whether agencies were in compliance with the requirement for fiscal year 2007, even though they are required by law to make such reports. According to agency officials, current systems are unable to track alternative fuel use at the level necessary to assess compliance. However, data from 2006 indicate that agencies primarily fueled their AFVs with gasoline—not alternative fuel—and our analysis found no evidence that this changed in 2007. Data reliability is a concern with respect to the third and fourth objectives. While about half of the agencies reported increasing their alternative fuel use by 10 percent and about two-thirds reported reducing petroleum use by 2 percent in 2007, persistent data problems call these results into question. Finally, no agency acquired plug-in hybrid electric vehicles because they were not commercially available.

Over the next few years, agencies will likely face challenges in meeting all but one of the fleet energy objectives. As they have over the past 4 years, agencies will likely continue to acquire the mandated percentage of AFVs. However, they will likely find it more difficult to meet both the requirement to fuel AFVs only with alternative fuel and the goal of increasing overall alternative fuel use by 10 percent annually because of the limited availability of alternative fuel. It is uncertain whether agencies will be able to reduce petroleum consumption annually by 2 percent in the near future, primarily because they will not be able to rely on alternative fuel to displace significant amounts of petroleum fuel. Furthermore, without better data, it will be difficult to judge agencies' progress in reducing petroleum consumption and increasing alternative fuel use.

Agency Performance in Meeting the Five Fleet Energy Objectives in Fiscal Year 2007

Source of objective	Fiscal year 2007 fleet energy objective	Number of agencies meeting objective	Percentage of agencies meeting objective
Energy Policy Act of 1992	*Requirement*: Acquire AFVs for 75 percent of new light-duty acquisitions by fleets of 20 or more vehicles in metropolitan statistical areas of 250,000 or more.	21	100
Energy Policy Act of 2005	*Requirement*: Must use only alternative fuel in AFVs. (DOE may waive the requirement if not feasible, which DOE defines to be if the fuel is unavailable within five miles or 15 minutes or costs 15 percent more than gasoline.)	0	0
Executive Order 13423	*Goal*: Increase overall alternative fuel use by at least 10 percent annually relative to the 2005 baseline	11	52
	Goal: Reduce petroleum consumption by 2 percent annually through fiscal year 2015 relative to the 2005 baseline	14	67
	Goal: Acquire plug-in hybrid electric vehicles when they are commercially available at a reasonable cost	0	0

Source: GAO analysis of DOE data.

Some agencies have taken steps to address these issues and improve data quality, but with limited success. Finally, agencies will not be able to meet the goal of acquiring plug-in hybrid electric vehicles until they become commercially available.

October 22, 2008

The Honorable Joseph I. Lieberman
Chairman
Committee on Homeland Security and Governmental Affairs
United States Senate

The Honorable Mark Pryor
United States Senate

The Honorable John Warner
United States Senate

Two-thirds of the oil consumed in the United States is used for transportation. The federal government's domestic vehicle fleet consists of about 600,000 civilianand nontactical military vehicles and consumes over 963,000 gallons of petroleum- based fuel per day. Although the federal fleet represents less than 1 percent of all vehicles on the road in the United States today, Congress and the administration have established energy conservation objectives for the federal fleet in an effort to provide leadership in reducing petroleum consumption. These objectives are established in federal law and executive orders and cover 21 federal agencies.[1] Agencies are required by law to

- acquire alternative fuel vehicles (AFV),[2] such as flex-fuel vehicles that can run either on gasoline or a blend of up to 85 percent ethanol and 15 percent gasoline (E85);[3] and
- fuel AFVs exclusively with alternative fuel,[4] unless exempted by waiver.

In addition, agencies are tasked by executive order to meet the goals of

- increasing overall alternative fuel use by at least 10 percent annually relative to their 2005 baseline;

- reducing petroleum consumption by 2 percent annually through fiscal year 2015 relative to their 2005 baseline; and
- acquiring plug-in hybrid electric vehicles when they are commercially available at a reasonable cost.[5]

Agencies are required to report annually on their progress in meeting the fleet energy objectives. These reports are to be made available on agencies' Web sites and are submitted to the Department of Energy (DOE), which is required to provide a comprehensive compliance report to Congress each year. Agencies also must respond to recommendations from both DOE and the Office of Management and Budget (OMB) that are designed to help agencies overcome barriers in meeting fleet objectives. These recommendations are provided through transportation management scorecards issued semiannually by DOE and OMB. Agencies also have to continually provide information on their fleets through DOE's Federal Analytical Statistical Tool (FAST) database, which is used, among other things, to collect information on agencies' alternative fuel vehicles, such as waiver requests to exempt vehicles when alternative fuel is not readily available or is too expensive. Finally, the Office of the Federal Environmental Executive (OFEE), located within the Environmental Protection Agency, also has a role in ensuring agencies' compliance with the fleet objectives. OFEE is responsible for administering the executive order governing the federal fleet, while DOE is primarily responsible for overseeing and administering the requirements under the law.

In this context, you asked us to determine (1) the extent to which agencies met the federal fleet energy objectives in fiscal year 2007 and (2) how agencies are poised to meet these objectives in the future. On September 4, 2008, we briefed staff of the committee on the results of our work. Enclosure I contains the briefing we used, with revisions to incorporate technical comments we subsequently received from the agencies involved. This correspondence summarizes the briefing, including the recommendations made to both DOE and GSA to help federal agencies meet fleet energy objectives. This correspondence also contains a matter for congressional consideration aimed at bringing to the attention of Congress possible inconsistencies between current energy objectives established in law and the availability of alternative fuel.

For the scope of this review, we included the 21 agencies and the corresponding domestic fleet vehicles for which DOE reports to Congress annually. To determine agencies' compliance with current federal fleet energy objectives, we relied primarily on information from DOE's FAST database.

We also conducted interviews with relevant fleet officials, including DOE officials and DOE's contractors that are responsible for FAST. To determine how agencies are poised to meet the fleet energy objectives in the future, we performed trend analyses using compliance data from FAST, analyzed transportation scorecards, and analyzed fleet data from FAST and the General Services Administration's (GSA) Special Order Program. We determined that the data we used were reliable for these purposes. More information on the scope and methods we used can be found in enclosure I.

Table 1. Agency Performance in Meeting the Fleet Energy Objectives, Fiscal Year 2007

Source of objective	Agencies' fiscal year 2007 fleet energy objective	Number of Agencies meeting objective	Percentage of agencies meeting objective
Energy Policy Act of 1992	*Requirement*: Acquire AFVs for 75 percent of new light-duty acquisitions by fleets of 20 or more vehicles in metropolitan statistical areas of 250,000 or more.	21	100
Energy Policy Act of 2005	*Requirement*: Must use only alternative fuel in AFVs. (DOE may waive requirement if operating on alternative fuel is not feasible, which DOE defines as fuel being unavailable within 5 miles or 15 minutes or costs 15 percent more than gasoline.)	0[a]	0[a]
Executive Order 13423	*Goal*: Increase overall alternative fuel use by at least 10 percent annually, relative to the 2005 baseline.	11	52
	Goal: Reduce petroleum consumption by 2 percent annually through fiscal year 2015, relative to the 2005 baseline.	14	67
	Goal: Acquire plug-in hybrid electric vehicles when they are commercially available at a reasonable cost.	0	0

Source: GAO analysis of DOE data.

[a] We estimated compliance for this objective in the aggregate only; not for each agency.

We conducted this performance audit from July 2007 through October 2008 in accordance with generally accepted government auditing standards.

Those standards require that we plan and perform the audit to obtain sufficient, appropriate evidence to provide a reasonable basis for our findings and conclusions based on our audit objectives. We believe that the evidence obtained provides a reasonable basis for our findings and conclusions based on our audit objectives.

RESULTS IN BRIEF

Federal agencies had mixed results in meeting the energy objectives for fleets in fiscal year 2007. First, all the agencies reported meeting or exceeding the requirement to acquire AFVs. However, they received some credit for AFVs not subject to the requirement, as allowed by DOE's implementing guidance. For example, only vehicles acquired inside large metropolitan areas are counted when establishing agencies' acquisition targets, but AFVs acquired outside those areas count toward meeting the targets. Second—regarding the requirement to use only alternative fuel in AFVs— neither DOE nor the agencies reported on whether agencies were in compliance with the requirement for 2007, even though they are required by law to make such reports. However, data from 2006 indicate that agencies primarily fueled their AFVs with gasoline—not alternative fuel—and our analysis found no evidence that this changed in 2007. Data reliability is a concern with respect to the third and fourth objectives. While about half of the agencies reported increasing their alternative fuel use by 10 percent and about two-thirds reported reducing petroleum use by 2 percent in 2007, persistent data problems call these results into question. Finally, no agency acquired plug-in hybrid electric vehicles because they were not commercially available.

Over the next few years, agencies will likely face challenges in meeting all but one of the fleet energy objectives. As they have over the past 4 years, agencies will likely continue to acquire the mandated percentage of AFVs. However, they will likely find it more difficult to meet both the requirement to fuel AFVs only with alternative fuel and the goal of increasing overall alternative fuel use by 10 percent annually because of the limited availability of alternative fuel. It is unclear whether agencies will be able to reduce petroleum consumption annually by 2 percent in the near future, primarily because they will not be able to rely on alternative fuel to displace significant amounts of petroleum fuel. Furthermore, without better data, it will be difficult to judge agencies' progress in increasing alternative fuel use and reducing petroleum consumption. Some agencies have taken steps to address these issues and improve data quality, but with limited success. Finally, agencies will not be able to meet the goal of acquiring plug-in hybrid electric vehicles until they become commercially available, which is not expected for several years.

More detailed information on each area we reviewed follows in Appendix I.

CONCLUSIONS

Allowing agencies to count AFV acquisitions that are not subject to the requirement toward meeting the requirement gives the incorrect impression that agencies are greatly exceeding the requirement. More importantly, agencies continue to acquire AFVs that they cannot expect to fuel with alternative fuel because of location or cost. They are fueling these vehicles mostly with petroleum, which does nothing to further the government's energy objectives. Until alternative fuel, particularly E85, is more widely available, agencies will likely continue to expend time and resources on acquiring AFVs with limited success in displacing petroleum, possibly missing opportunities to displace petroleum through other means. In addition, agencies and DOE have not met their clear responsibility to report on their compliance with the Energy Policy Act of 2005's alternative fueling requirement. Finally, in some cases, data quality problems have rendered agencies unable to accurately measure their progress toward the energy objectives.

RECOMMENDATIONS FOR EXECUTIVE ACTION

To accurately determine the progress agencies are making in meeting the requirement to use only alternative fuel in their AFVs, we are recommending that the Secretary of Energy report annually on agencies' compliance with the alternative fueling requirement of the EPAct. To provide information that more transparently captures agencies' compliance with the AFV acquisition requirement, we are recommending that the Secretary of Energy revise its implementation guidance to disallow AFV credits for AFVs not subject to the acquisition requirement. Because it is necessary to have accurate data for determining agencies' progress in increasing alternative fuel use and decreasing petroleum use, we also recommend that the Secretary of Energy and the Administrator of the General Services Administration continue their ongoing efforts to resolve data quality issues in these areas.

MATTER FOR CONGRESSIONAL CONSIDERATION

To help agencies more efficiently use their resources to increase use of alternative fuel and decrease use of petroleum, Congress should consider aligning the federal fleet AFV acquisition and fueling requirements with current alternative fuel availability and revising those requirements as appropriate.

APPENDIX I

BACKGROUND

Applicable Laws and Executive Order

- EPAct 1992 (as amended)
- Energy Conservation Reauthorization Act 1998
- EPAct 2005
- Executive Order 13423 (January 2007)

Coverage

- Twenty-one federal agencies with 20 or more domestic vehicles covered by the fleet requirements of the laws and executive order.
- All light-duty vehicles located in a metropolitan statistical area with population of 250,000 are subject to AFV acquisition objective (about 56 percent of domestic federal fleet in 2007).
- Waivers for the alternative fueling objective may be granted if operating the vehicle on alternative fuel is not feasible.

Fleet Subject to AFV Acquisition Objective, 2007

- 336,254 vehicles (see figure 1).

- Gasoline and E85 (a blend of about 85 percent ethanol and 15 percent gasoline) are the most common fuel types in the fleet (see figure 2).
- Ninety-nine percent of AFVs in the fleet are flex-fuel vehicles, which can operate on E85, regular gasoline, or any combination.

ESTABLISHMENT OF FEDERAL FLEET ENERGY OBJECTIVES

The Energy Policy Act (EPAct) of 1992 requires that 75 percent of all light-duty vehicles acquired starting in fiscal year 1999 be alternative fuel vehicles (AFV). The requirement covers fleets with 20 or more vehicles in the United States that are capable of being centrally fueled and operated in a metropolitan statistical area with more than 250,000 people. All light-duty vehicles that weigh 8,500 pounds or less are subject to this requirement. Certain law enforcement, emergency, and military tactical vehicles are exempt. In 2007, there were 336,254 vehicles that met this definition. Furthermore, in 1998, the Energy Conservation Reauthorization Act amended the EPAct to allow one AFV acquisition credit for each vehicle that operates solely on alternative fuel and one credit for every 450 gallons of biodiesel fuel used in vehicles over 8,500 pounds gross vehicle weight rating. These additional credits may not fulfill more than half of an agency's AFV requirement. The EPAct was again revised in 2005 to require that all AFVs be fueled with alternative fuel. Agencies may seek waivers from this requirement if operating the vehicles on alternative fuel is not feasible. The Department of Energy's (DOE) guidance stated this to be the case when alternative fuel is not available within 5 miles or 15 minutes of a vehicle's address or the cost exceeds that of conventional fuel by more than 15 percent. In 2007, Executive Order (E.O.) 13423, Strengthening Federal Environmental, Energy, and Transportation Management, added three goals to existing requirements. Under the new E.O., agencies are expected to (1) increase overall alternative fuel use by at least 10 percent annually relative to a 2005 baseline, (2) reduce petroleum use by 2 percent annually through fiscal year 2015, relative to a 2005 baseline, and (3) purchase plug-in hybrid electric vehicles when they are available at a reasonable cost.

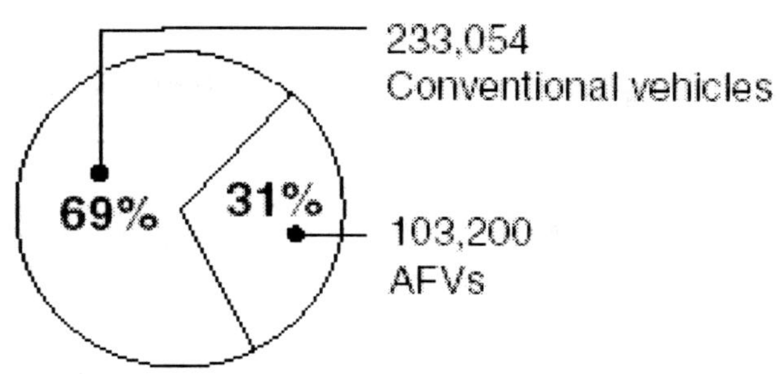

Source: GAO analysis of DOE fleet data.

Figure 1. Composition of Fleet Subject to AFV Acquisition Objective, Fiscal Year 2007

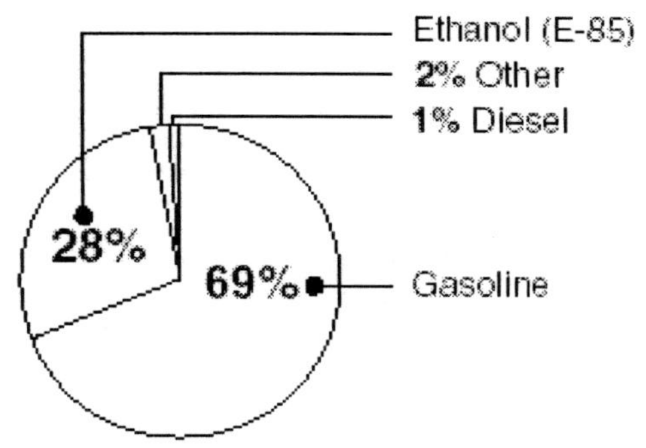

Source: GAO analysis of DOE fleet data.

Figure 2. Composition of Fleet Subject to AVF Acquisition Objective, by Fuel Type, Fiscal Year 2007

FLEET PERFORMANCE FY 2007

Fleet Energy Objective

#1. Seventy-five percent of new light-duty vehicles must be AFVs

FEDERAL AGENCIES HAD MIXED RESULTS IN MEETING THE ENERGY OBJECTIVES FOR THE FEDERAL FLEET IN 2007

Most Agencies Met the AFV Acquisition Requirement but Received Credit For AFVs That Were Not Subject to the Requirement

All 21 agencies (100 percent) reported meeting the AFV acquisition requirement in 2007.

Agencies acquired 59,832 total vehicles in 2007. Of these, 17,527 were light-duty vehicles subject to the AFV requirement and 42,305 were not. Thus, the target for 2007 was for agencies to acquire at least 13,145 AFVs (75 percent of 17,527).

- Of the 17,527 vehicle acquisitions subject to the requirement, agencies acquired 11,444 AFVs.
- Also, agencies will receive 3,878 additional credits toward meeting the requirement for acquiring AFVs that operate solely on alternative fuel, regardless of size, and for using biodiesel, as established by law.
- Furthermore, DOE's implementation guidance under the previous E.O. allowed agencies to count, or "credit," toward the target of 13,145 all the AFVs within the 59,832 vehicles they acquired—not just those within the 17,527 acquisitions that were subject to the fleet requirement. DOE's implementation of the new E.O. is ambiguous regarding these credits. If these credits are counted in 2007, agencies will receive credit for an additional 14,579 AFVs among the 42,305 acquisitions that were not subject to the fleet requirement— mostly for AFVs outside metropolitan areas—for a total of 26,023 AFV acquisitions.
- Combined, AFV acquisitions (26,023) and additional credits (3,878) would result in total AFV credits of 29,901. This amounts to 171 percent of the light-duty vehicle acquisitions covered by the EPAct 1992, well above the 75 percent requirement (see figure 3).

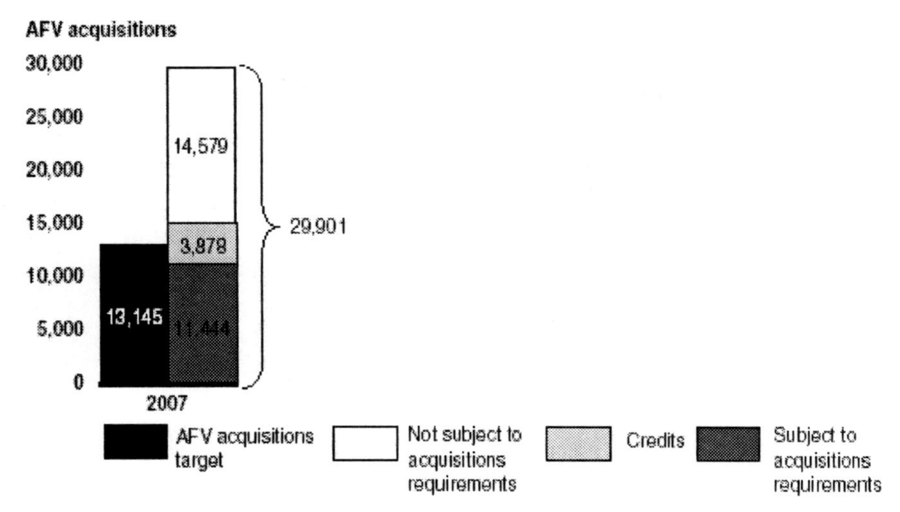

Source: GAO analysis of DOE fleet data.

Figure 3. AFV Acquisitions and Credits Earned, Fiscal Year 2007

#2. AFVs must be fueled with alternative fuel 100 percent of the time, unless they qualify for a waiver

DOE and Agencies Did Not Report on Agencies' Compliance with Alternative-Fuel-Only Fueling Requirement for 2007; However, Our Analysis Indicates That Agencies Did Not Meet the Requirement

Section 701 of EPAct 2005 directs DOE to monitor and report to Congress annually on agencies' compliance in fueling AFVs with alternative fuel 100 percent of the time, unless they qualify for a waiver because the fuel is not readily available or is too expensive.

- DOE did not compile or report compliance data relative to Section 701 in 2007 through its tracking and reporting system. However, for 2006, DOE reported on agencies' compliance with the executive order that preceded E.O. 13423, which set a goal for agencies to fuel AFVs with alternative fuel a majority of the time.

In 2006, DOE reported that none of the agencies met this goal, and collectively agencies fueled their AFVs with alternative fuel only about 7 percent of the time. Although DOE did not have data on alternative fuel use in AFVs for 2007, according to our analysis, results for 2007 would be similar to those for 2006

  - DOE did not require waivers for 2007 operations.
- Since 2006, agencies have been required to include information on their compliance with the EPAct 2005, as amended, including the requirement to fuel AFVs exclusively with alternative fuel, in their annual reports on their Web sites and in the *Federal Register.*
  - Our review of agencies' Web sites and the *Federal Register* in June 2008 found that many agencies' sites did not include updated annual reports, and several agencies had no annual reports at all. None of the 21 agencies reported on compliance with the EPAct requirement to fuel AFVs 100 percent of the time with alternative fuel in 2007.

#3. Increase overall alternative fuel use by 10 percent annually, relative to 2005 baseline

Over Half of the Agencies Reported Meeting the Goal of Increasing Their Use of Alternative Fuel by 10 Percent, but Data Are Unreliable

- Eleven of the 21 agencies (52 percent) reported meeting the goal. Collectively, agencies exceeded the alternative fuel target by over 461,000 gallons (about 7 percent). (See figure 4)
- According to DOE and other agency officials, data on alternative fuel use may be inaccurate due to problems associated with the tracking of alternative fuel. Most notably, fueling stations do not have standardized product codes for alternative fuel. Because most agencies rely on credit card records in reporting on the types and amounts of fuel they consume, determining the exact amount of alternative fuel, as well as petroleum fuel, used in their fleets can be a significant challenge.
  - DOE's annual 2006 report to Congress and the Office of the Federal Environmental Executive's 2007 report to the President

both noted inconsistencies in fuel consumption data provided by the agencies.

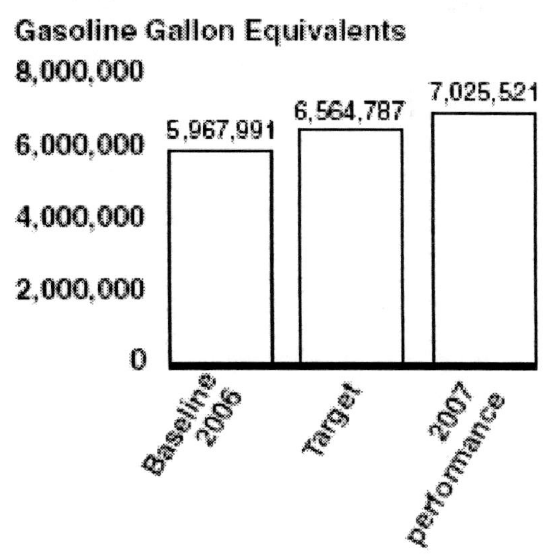

Source: GAO analysis of DOE fleet data.

Figure 4. Alternative Fuel Consumed by the Federal Fleet, Fiscal Year 2007

- Agency annual reports also cite continuous problems with tracking purchases of alternative fuel. Two agency officials told us they were unable to track and accurately report on alternative fuel use in their fleets. One fleet manager informed us that the amount of alternative fuel being used at one location was underreported by as much as 40 percent.
- The Office of Management and Budget (OMB) has cited inconsistent reporting in the annual transportation management scorecards it uses to assess agency compliance with fleet objectives. For example, in its 2007 scorecard for General Services Administration's (GSA) internal fleet, OMB commented on the inconsistency in the amounts of alternative fuel use reported by the agency in 2005 and 2006 (about 50,000 gallons in each year) relative to the amount reported in 2007 (about 2,200 gallons).

#4. Reduce petroleum consumption by 2 percent annually, relative to 2005 baseline

Two-Thirds of the Agencies Reported Meeting the Petroleum Reduction Goal, but the Data Are Unreliable

- Fourteen of the 21 agencies (67 percent) reported meeting the goal. Collectively, however, agencies fell short of the petroleum reduction target by about 167,000 gallons (see figure 5).
- The previous petroleum use goal was a 20 percent reduction by the end of fiscal year 2005 (about 3 percent annually) using 1999 as a baseline. No agency was able to meet that reduction goal. In 2007, according to DOE, the administration changed the goal to make it more achievable. Even under this relaxed target in 2007, one-third of the agencies and the federal government as a whole fell short of the goal.
- Data on petroleum consumption are unreliable, in part due to agencies' inability to accurately track alternative fuel use through credit card records:

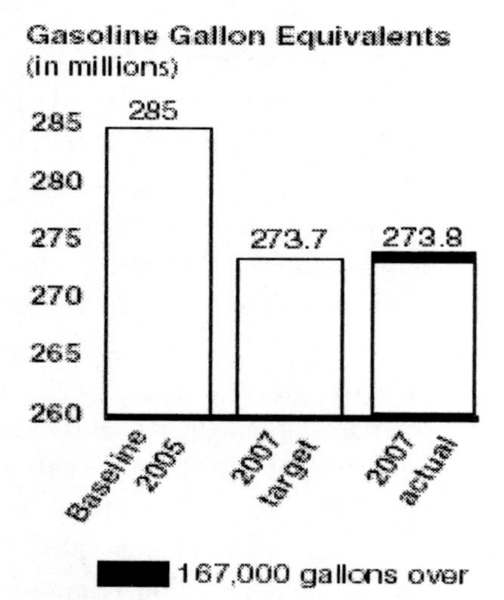

Source: GAO analysis of DOE fleet data.

Figure 5. Petroleum Fuel Consumption by the Federal Fleet in Fiscal Year 2007, Compared to the Fiscal Year 2007 Target for Reduction

- DOE's annual reports to Congress frequently cited concerns about the quality of petroleum consumption data provided by agencies.
- OMB, through its transportation scorecards, also has noted inconsistencies in agencies' data. For example, OMB commented on inaccuracies and inconsistencies found in fuel consumption and other data provided by the Department of Defense (DOD), GSA,[6] and the National Aeronautics and Space Administration (NASA).

#5. Acquire plug-in hybrid electric vehicles when commercially available and at a reasonable cost

Because of the Lack of Availability, No Agency Met the Goal to Acquire Plug-In Hybrid Electric Vehicles

- Agencies were not able to acquire plug-in hybrid electric vehicles because they were not commercially available.

PROJECTED PERFORMANCE

Fleet Energy Objective

#1. Seventy-five percent of new light-duty vehicles must be AFVs

AGENCIES WILL LIKELY FACE CHALLENGES IN MEETING ALL BUT ONE OF THE FLEET OBJECTIVES

Agencies Will Likely Continue to Meet AFV Acquisition Requirement in the Future

- In general, agencies have consistently exceeded the requirement for the past 3 years.

- About half of the agencies project that they will exceed their AFV acquisition targets in 2008.
- AFVs are readily available and are comparably priced to conventional vehicles.

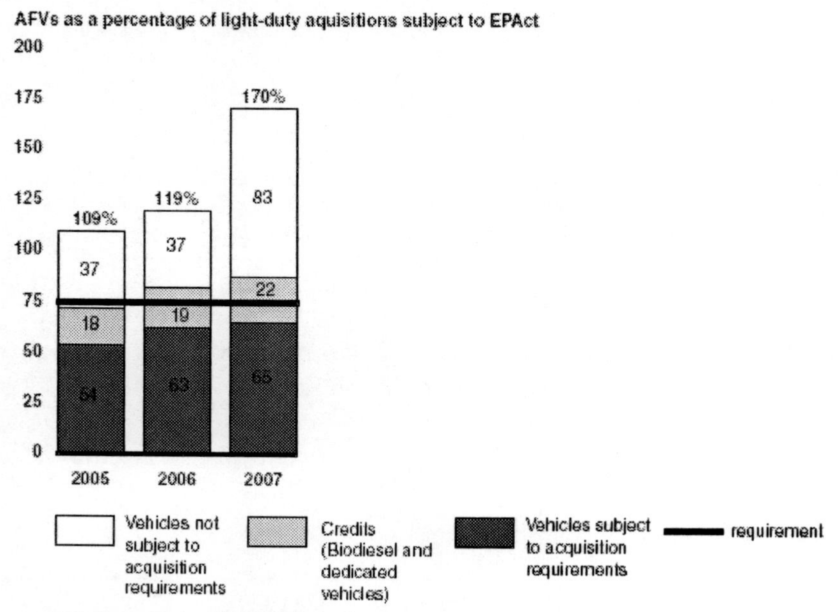

Source: GAO analysis of DOE fleet data.

Figure 6. Agency Performance in Meeting AFV Acquisition Requirement, Fiscal Years 2005-2007 (in percentage)

- According to DOE officials, agencies can count AFVs not subject to the requirement toward their AFV acquisition target. They also can receive additional credit for biodiesel use and for AFVs that operate only on alternative fuel. As a result, agencies have easily exceeded AFV acquisition targets for the past several years (see figure 6), even acquiring more AFVs in 2007 in areas not subject to the acquisition requirement than in those that were subject to it.

#2. AFVs must be fueled with alternative ful 100 with alternative fuel percent of the ime, 100 percent of t unless they qualify for a Waiver

Insufficient Alternative Fuel Infrastructure Will Likely Hinder Agencies' Ability to Fuel AFVs Exclusively with Alternative Fuel

Past performance strongly suggests that agencies will not achieve the requirement in the next few years.

- In the past 3 years, only two agencies met the alternative fueling requirement under the previous E.O., which called for agencies to fuel AFVs the majority of the time with alternative fuel. Collectively, agencies reported using alternative fuel in AFVs about 9 percent of the time in 2005 and 7 percent of the time in 2006. We estimate that agencies' alternative fuel use was about 8 percent in 2007.

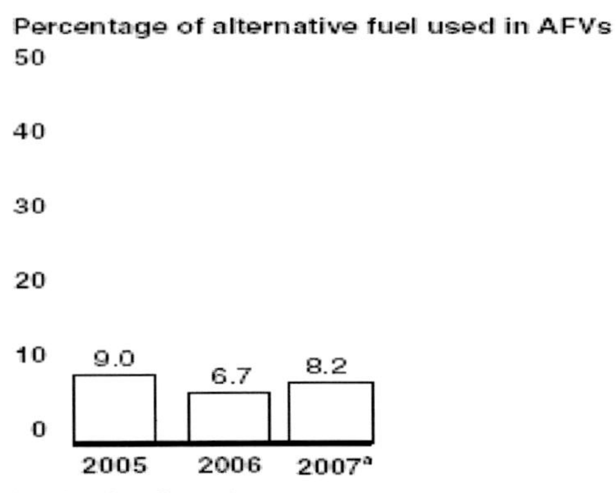

Source: GAO analysis of DOE fleet data.
[a]GAO estimated alternative fuel use in 2007.

Figure 7. Alternative Fuel Use in AFVs in Fiscal Years 2005, 2006, and 2007

- For 2008 operations, DOE assessed waiver requests submitted by the agencies. Eighteen of the 21 agencies requested waivers, primarily because the vehicles were not close enough to alternative fuel. DOE received waiver requests for 76,565 vehicles and approved 74,623 (97 percent), covering 61 percent of AFVs in the federal fleet.

Agencies face several barriers that may prevent them from achieving the requirement in the near future.

- Production levels of E85 are unlikely to increase significantly over the next few years because of limits to expanding U.S. ethanol production capacity and because less than 1 percent of that capacity is used in higher blends, such as in E85. (The most common use of corn ethanol is as a fuel extender in blends of 10 percent ethanol or less.)

- As of June 2008, only about 1,500 fueling stations nationwide, less than 1 percent, offered E85. Most are in the upper Midwest. Additionally, E85 is currently unavailable in 16 states, and 19 states have 10 public and federal fueling stations or fewer (see figure 8).

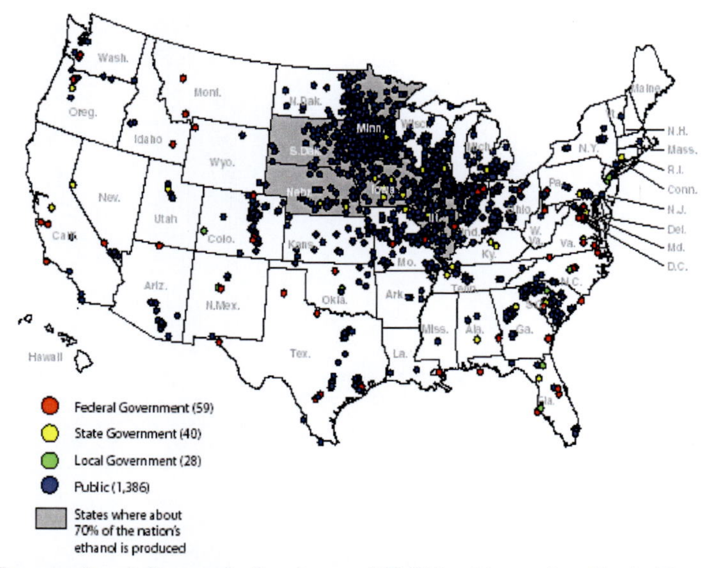

Source: Congressional Research Service and DOE's Alternative Fuels Data Center data.

Figure 8. Location of Government- and Private-Owned Fueling Stations Offering E85 as of June 2008

The agencies we reviewed have taken steps to increase their alternative fuel use:

- *Developed alternative fuel strategic action plans.* These incorporate partnering with other agencies and advocacy organizations in an effort to promote greater development of alternative infrastructure. For example, the GSA has partnered with DOE, the National Ethanol Vehicle Coalition, and other stakeholders to help industry identify potentially new alternative fueling locations.

- *Emphasized better communications.* For example, some agencies have made fleet training materials readily available to staff on their intranets and participate in periodic conference calls with national fleet transportation coordinators. Agencies also have shared their success stories through public and agency forums, such as work group meetings for federal agencies and annual federal fleet conferences.

- *Provided more accurate information.* Agencies provided information on the location of their AFVs to DOE's National Renewable Energy Laboratory (NREL), which uses this information to assist drivers in locating alternative fueling stations.

- *Increased the number of federal fueling stations offering E85.* For example, DOD has installed eight alternative fueling stations at various installations across the country. The Army is working with the Army Air Force Fuel Exchange Service to develop a business case for installing additional alternative fueling infrastructure. NASA has increased its E85 fueling capacity by adding an additional 10,000 gallon tank at Kennedy Space Center in Florida. An existing 1,000 gallon E85 tank at the Johnson Space Center in Texas will be relocated to make room for a 10,000 gallon E85 tank, and NASA's White Sands Test Facility in New Mexico has activated a 2,500 gallon E85 tank.

#3. Increase overall alternative fuel use by 10 percent annually, relative to the 2005 baseline

Insufficient Infrastructure Will Also Likely Hinder Agencies from Increasing Their Use of Alternative Fuel by 10 Percent Annually

As with the previous requirement, agencies' ability to meet this goal will be significantly hampered by the limited availability of alternative fuel.

- Limited fueling stations and low production levels of E85 will limit the amount of alternative fuel available to agencies.

- Concerns over data reliability will likely continue to make it difficult to accurately assess agencies' compliance.

Agencies have taken steps to improve data quality.

- *Improved the tracking of alternative fuel.* For example, GSA has improved its Fleet Drive Thru, a Web-based data collection and reporting system for vehicles leased through GSA. Among other things, the system allows agencies to retrieve fueling data for AFVs directly, allowing for inaccuracies to be more readily identified.

- *Increased external efforts to improve data quality.* For example, GSA, DOE, and the National Ethanol Vehicle Coalition have partnered to urge the fuel industry to standardize fuel product codes and to assist credit card providers in resolving errors in their reports on alternative fuel purchases.

#4. Reduce petroleum consumption by 2 percent annually, relative to 2005 baseline

Agencies' Prospects for Significantly Reducing Petroleum Use in the Future Are Uncertain

Agencies face difficulties in continuing to meet the petroleum reduction goal.

- About 99 percent of the ethanol produced in the United States is used in blends of 10 percent or less, limiting the government's ability to significantly displace petroleum.
- AFVs can be more costly to buy and operate than standard vehicles. The U.S. Postal Service, which owns the largest number of E85 vehicles of any agency—about 37,000 in 2007—found that these vehicles are more costly to buy and operate than non-AFVs because of the higher fuel cost of E85 and lower fuel efficiency of AFVs. The Postal Service reported that their AFVs reduced fuel efficiency by about 29 percent, thereby increasing fuel consumption by about 1.5 million gallons in 2007.

- A limited number of fuel-efficient AFVs are available to agencies. We found that from 2006 through 2008, GSA offered through its Special Order Program, the means by which most agencies acquire vehicles, only one AFV compact sedan—a 6-cylinder model—and no subcompact AFV sedans. According to GSA officials, the program includes the most fuel-efficient AFVs available commercially—automobile manufacturers currently offer few fuel-efficient AFVs. GSA officials pointed out that agencies may acquire vehicles outside of the program, but agencies will typically pay significantly more for these vehicles.

Rather than relying on E85, some agencies have turned to other methods to reduce petroleum use.

- *Increased their use of conventional hybrids*. The Postal Service and other agencies are using conventional hybrids in an effort to reduce petroleum consumption. Postal Service officials believe that hybrids are better suited for stop-and-go driving by service carriers and can improve fuel efficiency by as much as 21 percent. EPAct 1992 was amended in 2008 to include conventional hybrids in the definition of AFVs; however, the additional cost of hybrids, $8,000 to $10,000 per vehicle, also may limit agencies' use of them.

- *Employed better fleet management practices*. Several agencies have reduced the number of vehicles in their fleets, encouraged carpooling, and instructed drivers to take actions aimed at increasing fuel efficiency, such as observing posted speed limits and performing scheduled maintenance.
- *Leveraged resources to acquire other types of AFVs*. NASA partnered with the Marine Corps to urge GSA to acquire about 40 compressed natural gas vehicles through a special purchase arrangement between GSA and Honda.

- *Studied ways to reduce petroleum consumption*. NASA has begun testing electric vehicles, the Postal Service is continuing its test of conventional hybrids, and GSA is trying to identify vehicles it could replace with more fuel-efficient models.

Projected Performance

Fleet Energy Objective

#5. Acquire plug-in hybrid electric vehicles when commercially available and at a reasonable cost

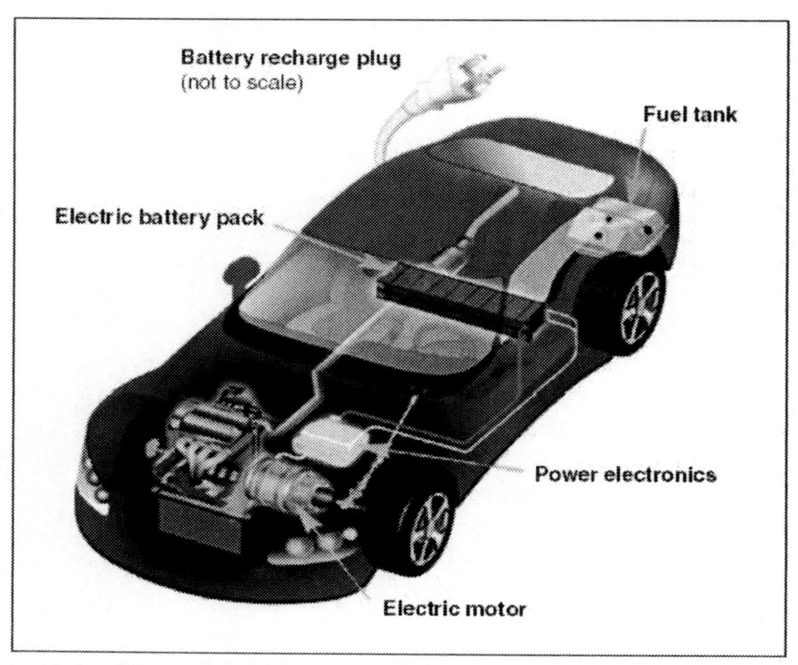

Source: National Renewable Energy Laboratory for Department of Energy.

Figure 9. Components of a Plug-in Hybrid Electric Vehicle

Plug-In Hybrid Electric Vehicles Are Unlikely to Be Widely Available Before 2010 at the Earliest

- Battery weight, durability, and cost are the biggest obstacles to commercializing plug-in hybrid electric vehicles. Limited production by Toyota and General Motors might begin in 2010.
- In July 2008, GAO initiated a review regarding issues associated with using plug-in hybrid electric vehicles in the federal government.

CONCLUSIONS AND RECOMMENDATIONS

Conclusions

Since 1992, Congress and the President have sought to reduce federal dependence on petroleum, using alternative fuel as one of their main tools. Virtually every agency has succeeded in acquiring more AFVs, but none has been able to significantly displace petroleum with alternative fuel, due to its lack of availability. Furthermore, allowing agencies to count AFV acquisitions that are not subject to the requirement toward meeting the requirement gives the incorrect impression that agencies are greatly exceeding the requirement. More importantly, agencies continue to acquire AFVs that they cannot expect to fuel with alternative fuel because of location or cost. Instead, they are fueling these vehicles mostly with gasoline, which does nothing to further the government's energy objectives. In some cases, it has increased total fuel consumption, making operation of the vehicles more costly than if the agency had purchased standard vehicles. Until alternative fuel, particularly E85, is more widely available, agencies will likely continue to expend time and resources on acquiring AFVs with limited success in displacing petroleum. In places where agencies do not have a reasonable prospect of achieving the fueling requirement, they may miss opportunities to displace petroleum consumption through other means. Petroleum reduction is one of the central rationales behind all five energy objectives. However, the acquisition and fueling requirements may, in some cases, undermine efforts to cut petroleum use. In addition, agencies and DOE have not met their clear responsibility to report on their compliance with the EPAct's 2005 alternative fueling requirement. Furthermore, in some cases, data quality problems have rendered agencies unable to accurately measure their progress toward increasing alternative fuel or reducing petroleum consumption, or to effectively target areas for improvement.

Recommendations for Executive Action

We recommend that the Secretary of Energy (1) report annually on agencies' compliance with the alternative fueling requirement under Section 701 of EPAct 2005, and (2) revise DOE's implementation guidance to disallow AFV credits for AFVs not subject to the acquisition requirement.

We recommend that the Secretary of Energy and the Administrator of the General Services Administration continue their ongoing efforts to resolve data quality issues in these areas.

Comments from the General Services Administration

GSA Administrator

September 26, 2008

The Honorable Gene L. Dodaro
Acting Comptroller General
U.S. Government Accountability Office
Washington, DC 20548

Dear Mr. Dodaro:

The U.S. General Services Administration (GSA) thanks you for the opportunity to review and comment on the draft report, "FEDERAL ENERGY MANAGEMENT: Agencies Are Acquiring Alternative Fuel Vehicles but Face Challenges in Meeting Other Fleet Objectives" (GAO-08-1112R). We concur with the joint recommendation to the Department of Energy (DOE) and GSA, and we will continue our ongoing work with DOE to resolve data quality issues.

If you have any questions, please contact me. Staff inquiries may be directed to Mr. Kevin Messner, Associate Administrator, Office of Congressional and Intergovernmental Affairs, at (202) 501-0563.

Sincerely,

James A. Williams
Acting Administrator

cc: Mark Gaffigan, Director, Natural Resources and Environment, GAO

Matter for Congressional Consideration

Congress should consider aligning the federal fleet AFV acquisition and fueling requirements with current alternative fuel availability and revising those requirements as appropriate.

End Notes

[1] The Energy Policy Act of 1992, as amended, and Executive Order 13423 establish the federal agencies that are subject to fleet energy requirements and goals. These agencies must have 20 or more domestic vehicles, and include: Court Services and Offender Supervision Agency for the District of Columbia; General Services Administration; National Aeronautics and Space Administration; Smithsonian Institute; Social Security Administration; Departments of Agriculture, Commerce, Defense, Energy, Health and Human Services, Homeland Security, Housing and Urban Development, Interior, Justice, Labor, State, Transportation, Treasury, and Veterans Affairs; Environmental Protection Agency; and U.S. Postal Service.

[2] Under the Energy Policy Act of 1992, as amended, AFVs include any dedicated, flexible-fuel, or dual- fuel vehicle designed to operate on at least one alternative fuel. In 2008, EPAct was amended to include conventional hybrids.

[3] The alternative fuel acquisition requirement applies only to light-duty vehicles capable of being centrally fueled and operated in metropolitan statistical areas of more than 250,000 people.

[4] Alternative fuels under DOE regulations include: methanol, ethanol, and other alcohols; blends of 85 percent or more of alcohol with gasoline; natural gas and liquid fuels domestically produced from natural gas; liquefied petroleum gas (propane); coal-derived liquid fuels; hydrogen; electricity; biodiesel; and p-series fuels. 10 C.F.R. § 490.2.

[5] The Energy Independence and Security Act, Pub. L. No. 110-140 (2007), added petroleum reduction and alternative fuel requirements. Specifically, the Act requires that not later than 2015 and each year thereafter, agencies achieve a 20 percent reduction in annual petroleum consumption and a 10 percent increase in alternative fuel consumption relative to a 2005 baseline; also, that agencies begin by 2010 to reduce petroleum consumption and increase alternative fuel consumption at a rate that will enable them to meet these requirements. We did not include the new law in the scope of our study because the law was passed in fiscal year 2008, which is beyond the time frame covered by this report (agency performance for 2007).

[6] We refer to GSA's internal fleet of about 1,200 vehicles.

In: Federal Energy Management and Government... ISBN: 978-1-60692-985-8
Editor: Amelia R. Williams

Chapter 2

FEDERAL ENERGY MANAGEMENT ADDRESSING CHALLENGES THROUGH BETTER PLANS AND CLARIFYING THE GREENHOUSE GAS EMISSION MEASURE WILL HELP MEET LONG-TERM GOALS FOR BUILDINGS*

U.S. Government Accountability Office

WHY GAO DID THIS STUDY

The federal government is the nation's single largest energy consumer, spending approximately $17 billion in fiscal year 2007. A number of statutes and executive orders have established and revised goals directing agencies to reduce energy consumption and greenhouse gas emissions—such as carbon dioxide, which results from combustion of fossil fuels and natural processes, among other things—and increase renewable energy use. GAO was asked to determine the extent to which (1) federal agencies met energy efficiency, greenhouse gas emission, and renewable energy goals in fiscal year 2007; (2)

---

* This is an edited, reformatted and augmented version of a U. S. Government Accountability Office publication dated September 2008.

federal agencies have made progress in each of these areas in the recent past; and (3) six selected agencies are poised to meet energy goals into the future. For this review, GAO, among other things, conducted site visits for six agencies and reviewed the Department of Energy's (DOE) annual reports to Congress on federal energy management.

WHAT GAO RECOMMENDS

GAO recommends that DOE (1) reevaluate the current measure for greenhouse gas emissions and establish one that more accurately reflects agencies' performance in reducing these emissions, and (2) finalize and issue guidance for agencies' use in developing long-term plans that contains key elements for meeting current and future energy goals. GSA, NASA, and USPS concurred; VA neither agreed nor disagreed; and the other agencies did not comment.

WHAT GAO FOUND

Based on draft DOE data, most of the 22 agencies reporting to DOE for fiscal year 2007 met energy goals for energy efficiency, greenhouse gas emissions, and renewable energy. Specifically, all but one agency met the energy efficiency goal. Three of these agencies would not have met the goal through reductions in energy intensity—the amount of energy consumed per gross square foot—alone; they also used credits for the purchase of renewable energy or source energy to help meet the goal. Because the greenhouse gas emission goal is tied to the energy efficiency goal, the same number of agencies met the greenhouse gas emission goal, while 17 of the 22 agencies met the renewable energy goal.

Determining the extent to which agencies have made progress over time toward the goals is problematic due to key changes in the goals—as specified in statute and executive order—and how progress is measured. For example, the energy efficiency goal changed the types of buildings included and the baseline year against which progress was measured. The greenhouse gas emissions goal also changed, from a measure of greenhouse gas emissions to a measure of energy intensity; this change makes it problematic to compare performance before and after the change. Moreover, GAO found that a goal based on energy intensity is not a good proxy for emissions because a reduction in energy intensity does not always result in lower greenhouse gas emissions. Although there is no consensus on a best measure at present, alternative measures are in use that may better track agencies' greenhouse gas emissions than the current measure based on energy intensity.

Agencies' prospects for meeting energy goals into the future depend on overcoming four key challenges. First, the six agencies GAO reviewed—the departments of Defense (DOD), Energy (DOE), and Veterans Affairs (VA); the General Services Administration (GSA); the National Aeronautics and Space Administration (NASA); and the U.S. Postal Service (USPS)—had long-term plans for achieving energy goals that lacked key elements, such as plans that outline agencies' strategies that are linked to goals and provide a framework for aligning activities, processes, and resources to attain the goals of the plan. Second, investment in energy projects competes with other budget priorities, causing agency officials to increasingly rely on alternative financing mechanisms—contracts with private companies that pay for energy improvements. However, as past GAO work has shown, agencies entering into these contracts could not always verify whether money saved from using less energy was greater than projected costs and may yield lower savings than if timely, full, and upfront appropriations had been used. Third, agencies face challenges in obtaining reliable energy consumption data but are taking steps to collect more reliable data. Finally, facilities may lack staff dedicated to energy management and may find it difficult to retain staff with sufficient energy expertise; however, agency officials are participating in training and implementing initiatives for energy management personnel.

ABBREVIATIONS

ASE	Alliance to Save Energy
Btu	British thermal unit
DOD	Department of Defense
DOE	Department of Energy
EISA 2007	Energy Independence and Security Act of 2007
E.O. 13123	Executive Order 13123
E.O. 13423	Executive Order 13423
EPA	Environmental Protection Agency
EPAct 2005	Energy Policy Act of 2005

ESPC	energy savings performance contract
GSA	General Services Administration
NASA	National Aeronautics and Space Administration
OFEE	Office of the Federal Environmental Executive
OMB	Office of Management and Budget
REC	renewable energy certificate
UESC	utility energy savings contract
USPS	U.S. Postal Service
VA	Department of Veterans Affairs

September 30, 2008
The Honorable Joseph I. Lieberman
Chairman
Committee on Homeland Security and Governmental Affairs
United States Senate

The Honorable Mark Pryor
United States Senate

The Honorable John Warner
United States Senate

The federal government is the nation's single largest energy consumer, spending approximately $17 billion in fiscal year 2007 on energy for buildings and vehicles, according to the most recent available data. This total represents almost 1 percent of all federal expenditures for 2007. And these costs have been rising in recent years. According to the Department of Energy (DOE), from 2003 to 2007, the cost per unit of energy increased by 59 percent in constant 2007 dollars. In light of these energy price increases, congressional interest in making the federal government more energy efficient has grown as well.

Statute or executive order	Building categories	Energy efficiency	Greenhouse gas emissions	Renewable energy
E.O. 13123 (June 3, 1999)	Standard buildings	Each agency is to reduce energy consumption per gross square foot of its facilities by 30% by 2005 and 35% by 2010, compared to 1985	Each agency is to reduce greenhouse gas emissions attributed to building energy use by 30% by 2010 compared with such emissions levels in 1990	By 2005, 2.5% of building electricity consumption shall come from renewable energy projects (electric or thermal/gas) built after 1990[a]
	Industrial/laboratory buildings	Each agency is to reduce energy consumption per square foot, per unit of production, or per other unit as applicable by 20% by 2005 and 25% by 2010, relative to 1990	Same as for standard buildings	Same as for standard buildings
EPAct 2005 (August 8, 2005)	All buildings	Reduce energy consumption per gross square foot by 2% annually in fiscal years 2006 through 2015, relative to a 2003 baseline		Of the total amount of electric energy an agency consumes, the following amounts are to be from renewable electric energy: not less than: 3% in FY 2007-2009, 5% in FY 2010-2012, 7.5% in FY 2013 and beyond (no new source requirement – i.e., projects built after a certain date)
E.O. 13423 (January 24, 2007)	All buildings	Reduce energy intensity by (i) 3% annually through the end of FY 2015 or (ii) 30% by the end of FY 2015, relative to the baseline of the agency's energy use in 2003	Reduce greenhouse gas emissions through a reduction of energy intensity of (i) 3% annually through the end of FY 2015 or (ii) 30% by the end of FY 2015, relative to the agency's energy use in 2003	At least half of the renewable energy required in EPAct 2005 consumed by an agency in a fiscal year should come from new renewable resources (those placed in service after January 1, 1999)

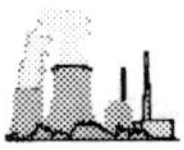

Sources: GAO analysis of EPAct 2005 and EOs 13123 and 13423; Art Explosion (clip art).

Note: Buildings meeting certain criteria—such as those with a national security function—may be excluded from meeting the energy goals.

[a]Section 503 of E.O. 13123 directed the Secretary of Energy, in collaboration with the heads of other agencies, to develop goals for the amount of energy generated at federal facilities from renewable energy technologies. In July 2000, the Secretary approved the goal specifying that 2.5 percent of building electricity consumption shall come from renewable energy projects built after 1990.

Figure 1. Changes to Energy Efficiency, Greenhouse Gas Emissions, and Renewable Energy Goals, Fiscal Years 1999–2007

Since the 1970s, federal statutes and executive orders have set and revised a number of goals for changing the way federal agencies use or obtain energy. Most recently, the Energy Policy Act of 2005 (EPAct 2005) and two executive orders set energy goals for federal agencies. As figure 1 shows, the goals address such areas as improving energy efficiency, reducing greenhouse gas emissions,[1] and increasing the use of renewable energy sources.[2] For greenhouse gas emissions, Executive Order 13423 (E.O. 13423) lays out a direction linked to the energy efficiency goal rather than a numerical goal specific to emissions.[3] These goals apply to a range of buildings, from standard office buildings to more energy-intensive buildings, such as industrial or laboratory buildings.[4] In January 2007, E.O. 13423 revoked Executive Order 13123 (E.O. 13123), which had guided agencies in energy conservation efforts since June 1999 and added energy goals to those in EPAct 2005.[5,6] In addition, the statute and E.O. 13423 set goals for agencies to reduce petroleum consumption and increase the use of alternative fuels in vehicle fleets. Some types of federal buildings are excluded from these goals, such as buildings for which national security is overwhelmingly the primary function and prevents the implementation of energy efficiency measures or prohibits reporting of energy data because it would pose a demonstrated security risk.

As figure 1 shows, EPAct 2005 changed the energy efficiency goal in E.O. 13123. Further, the most recent executive order, E.O. 13423, increased the reduction in energy intensity called for in EPAct 2005. Energy intensity is the amount of energy consumed—measured in British thermal units (Btu)—per gross square foot. The energy goals in place for the agencies in fiscal year 2007 are the following:

- *Energy efficiency*. Reduce energy intensity by 6 percent, from a 2003 baseline. EPAct 2005 required a 2 percent annual reduction in energy intensity starting in 2006, which would have resulted in a total of 4 percent for 2007. However, the new executive order was implemented mid-fiscal year 2007, and the implementation instructions for the new order directed agencies to reduce energy intensity by 6 percent for fiscal year 2007, from a 2003 baseline. After 2007, E.O. 13423 directs agencies to reduce energy intensity by 3 percent annually, or a total of 30 percent by the end of fiscal year 2015, relative to a 2003 baseline. Agencies could count two types of credits toward their energy efficiency goal in fiscal year 2007: credits for purchasing renewable energy and source energy credits. To calculate credits for purchasing renewable energy, DOE subtracts a purchase from the amount of energy the agency consumes in measuring its progress toward the goal.[7] This credit will be phased out completely by fiscal year 2012. Source energy credits take into account the use of site energy—energy used only at a particular site—and source energy—the energy consumed in producing and delivering energy to the site. For example, an agency can obtain source credits if it generates electricity on-site using natural gas and recovers the heat used to generate the electricity. While the agency may use more site energy, it reduces its electricity purchases and the use of associated fuels at the power plant, thereby decreasing total energy use. According to DOE, these credits are expected to continue as a necessary adjustment for the site-delivered Btu-per-gross-square-foot performance measure.

- *Greenhouse gas emissions*. Reduce greenhouse gas emissions by reducing energy intensity by 6 percent by 2007, from a 2003 baseline. After 2007, agencies are to reduce greenhouse gas emissions by reducing energy intensity by 3 percent annually, or a total of 30 percent by the end of fiscal year 2015, relative to a 2003 baseline.

- *Renewable energy*. Of the total amount of electricity consumed, at least 3 percent must be from a renewable energy source, with at least half of that amount from a renewable energy source put into service after January 1, 1999. This goal is in place through 2009. After 2009, the percentage of electricity from a renewable energy source increases incrementally, but at least half of the amount must still be from renewable energy sources put into service after January 1, 1999.[8] Under EPAct 2005, agencies also get a 100 percent bonus for renewable electric energy generated on federal or Indian land. Under E.O. 13423, this energy must be defined as "new" to qualify for the bonus.

DOE, the Office of the Federal Environmental Executive (OFEE), and the Office of Management and Budget (OMB) play a role in ensuring that agencies comply with the goals. DOE is responsible primarily for coordinating the implementation of the energy efficiency and renewable energy goals for agencies set forth in EPAct 2005, while OFEE is responsible primarily for overseeing the implementation of E.O. 13423. In practice, OFEE has delegated much of its responsibility for achieving federal energy goals to DOE. OMB is responsible for, among other things, issuing semiannual scorecards that track agencies' energy performance for a number of indicators.

DOE develops and issues guidance on how to meet the energy goals. It also chairs the Interagency Energy Management Task Force, a group of agency headquarters-level energy managers who, among other things, address energy issues affecting federal buildings and operations and comment on guidance. DOE also reports annually to Congress on agencies' energy use and progress toward meeting energy goals. Not all agencies report every year, and the agencies reporting may vary from year to year; however, the majority of federal agencies report each year. In some cases, when control of a building is delegated from the General Services Administration (GSA) to an agency, the agency will then be required to report to DOE, which may influence the number of agencies included in the annual report.

To achieve the energy goals, agencies may take a range of actions, from switching to more energy-efficient lighting and encouraging staff to conserve energy, to ensuring that all new building construction meets higher energy efficiency standards. Agencies pay for these improvements in several ways; for example, they may use upfront funding to pay for the improvements outright or they may rely on alternative financing mechanisms, such as contracts with private companies that pay for energy improvements to begin with and then receive compensation from the agencies over time from the monetary savings they realize from these projects.

In this context, you asked us to determine the extent to which (1) federal agencies met energy efficiency, greenhouse gas emission, and renewable energy goals in fiscal year 2007; (2) federal agencies have made progress in each of these areas in the recent past; and (3) selected agencies are poised to meet energy goals into the future. We plan to report in fall 2008 on energy efforts related to the federal government's vehicle fleets.

To determine the extent to which agencies met energy efficiency, greenhouse gas, and renewable energy goals, we analyzed data on agencies' performance, as reported in DOE's annual reports to Congress for fiscal year 2005, and draft data from fiscal years 2006 and 2007. We determined these data to be sufficiently reliable for our purpose, which was to convey what the agencies reported to DOE about the status of meeting the energy goals. To assess the agencies' progress in each of these areas in recent years, we reviewed energy efficiency, greenhouse gas, and renewable energy goals in current and previous statutes and executive orders. We also met with officials from DOE, OFEE, and OMB to gain their perspective on the goals. To determine the extent to which the agencies are poised to meet future energy goals, we selected six agencies on the basis of several factors, such as the agencies' combined energy consumption as a percentage of the federal government's consumption (nearly 94 percent in fiscal year 2005). Because these six agencies accounted for nearly 94 percent of the energy consumed in standard buildings in fiscal year 2005, our findings for these agencies may have great implications for the federal government as a whole. The selected agencies are the Departments of Defense (DOD)—Air Force, Army, and the

Department of Navy—Energy, and Veterans Affairs (VA); GSA; the National Aeronautics and Space Administration (NASA); and the U.S. Postal Service (USPS). We obtained documentation and met with headquarters officials from these six agencies. We visited a minimum of two sites per agency to determine their efforts toward meeting energy goals at the local level. We also met with officials from the Alliance to Save Energy (ASE), a nonprofit organization recognized for its work on energy issues. Appendix I contains a more detailed discussion of our scope and methodology. We conducted this performance audit from May 2007 through September 2008 in accordance with generally accepted government auditing standards. Those standards require that we plan and perform the audit to obtain sufficient, appropriate evidence to provide a reasonable basis for our findings and conclusions based on our audit objectives. We believe that the evidence obtained provides a reasonable basis for our findings and conclusions based on our audit objectives.

RESULTS IN BRIEF

Most of the 22 agencies reporting to DOE for fiscal year 2007 met their energy-related goals, according to draft data supplied by the agencies. All but 1 agency met the energy efficiency goal of a 6 percent reduction in energy intensity from a 2003 baseline. Because the greenhouse gas emission direction is tied to the energy efficiency goal, all but 1 agency also met the greenhouse gas emissions goal of a 6 percent reduction in energy intensity from a 2003 baseline. Three agencies used renewable energy purchase or source energy credits to meet the goals and would not have met the goals through reductions in energy intensity alone. Seventeen of the 22 agencies met the renewable energy goal of having 3 percent of their electricity consumption from renewable resources, with at least half of this amount from renewable sources placed into service after January 1, 1999.

Assessing the extent to which agencies have made progress over time toward the goals of increasing energy efficiency, reducing greenhouse gas emissions, or increasing the use of renewable energy is problematic due to key changes in the energy goals and how the goals are measured—as specified in statute and executive order. For example, before 2006, buildings subject to the energy efficiency goal were divided into two categories—one for standard buildings measured against a 1985 baseline and one for industrial and laboratory buildings measured against a 1990 baseline—but the goal for 2006 onward is based only on one building category measured against a 2003 baseline. As a result, comparing agency performance in meeting the goal before and after 2006 is problematic and does not meaningfully describe energy efficiency progress toward the goal over time. In the case of greenhouse gas emissions, measurement is even more complex. The 2007 executive order not only changed the baseline year but also fundamentally changed what is being measured. Before 2007, the greenhouse gas emissions goal, set in 1999 by executive order, was to reduce the amount of emissions, which is significantly different from the energy-intensity-based goal for 2007 onward. In fact, the goal the administration established in the executive order may not accurately reflect progress toward the goal of reducing greenhouse gas emissions. That is, energy intensity is not always a good proxy for emissions depending on, among other things, the energy sources used. For example, if an agency's square footage and energy consumption remain constant while the agency switches to sources with greater greenhouse gas emissions, its energy intensity remains constant while the greenhouse gas emissions increase. In fact, we found instances in which agencies' energy intensity decreased while their greenhouse gas emissions increased. While an energy-intensity-based goal, such as the current goal under the 2007 executive order, does not always indicate progress toward the goal of reducing greenhouse gas emissions, there is no consensus on a best measure at present; however, there are alternative measures that may better track agencies' greenhouse gas emissions than the current measure based on energy intensity.

The prospects for meeting energy goals into the future for the six agencies we examined depend largely on addressing four key challenges: (1) lack of key elements in long-term plans that would help provide agency direction, (2) budget constraints for energy projects, (3) measurement and data reliability issues, and (4) lack of expertise and dedicated energy management staff. However, agencies are planning to meet energy goals by undertaking several activities to address these four challenges.

- *Long-term plans lack key elements.* Long-term plans can help clarify organizational priorities and unify agency staff in the pursuit of shared goals. As previous GAO work has shown, such plans should, among other things, outline agency strategies that are linked to goals and provide a framework for aligning agency activities, processes, and resources to attain the goals of the plan; identify the resources needed; and provide for reliable performance data needed to set goals, evaluate results, and improve performance.[9] The long-term plans for the six agencies we reviewed lack many of these key elements. Furthermore, four of the six agencies have not updated their plans to reflect the goals set out by E.O. 13423. DOE has drafted guidance for agencies on developing long-term plans that addresses most of the key elements we identified. This guidance will be published in final form upon completion of DOE internal review and reconciliation with new planning requirements in the Energy Independence and Security Act of 2007 (EISA 2007). In the absence of long-term plans, agency officials reported using several tools to meet energy goals, including short-term plans for energy improvements, as well as energy audits to identify and plan future energy projects. However, these tools do not focus on efforts to meet the energy goals through fiscal year 2015 and may not ensure that agencies will meet these goals.

- *Constrained budgets limit energy projects.* According to agency officials, meeting long-term energy goals will require major initial capital investment, but such investments must compete with other budget priorities. To overcome budget constraints, and, partly in response to administration guidance, officials are increasingly turning to alternative financing mechanisms that primarily rely on third parties to fund projects, with the promise that the agency will repay the third parties from energy savings. This approach offers benefits and presents challenges. For example, according to DOD officials, the department needs these mechanisms to achieve long-term energy goals, but these mechanisms can take a long time to implement and require contracting and oversight expertise not always available on-site. In addition, as previous GAO work has shown, agencies entering into these contracts could not always verify whether money saved from using less energy was greater than projected costs and may yield lower savings than if timely, full, and upfront appropriations had been used.[10] Some agencies are undertaking initiatives, such as centralizing the contracting process for energy projects, to overcome challenges associated with alternative financing.

- *Measurement and data reliability issues.* Reliable data are essential to making decisions. Currently, however, some agencies estimate energy use from monthly bills, handwritten ledgers, or other sources that may not be reliable. To address this challenge, agencies have and are pursuing some mechanisms to improve data reliability. For example, all of the six agencies we met with plan to install advanced electrical meters on buildings by 2012, as required by EPAct 2005.

- *Some sites lack expertise and dedicated energy management staff.* Complex energy projects may require high levels of expertise and dedicated energy management staff. However, according to officials at several of the sites we visited, they do not have a full-time energy manager and lack staff with expertise in negotiating and overseeing alternative financing mechanisms, both of which hinder their efforts to meet energy goals. In addition, several sites have had difficulty retaining qualified and experienced personnel to manage energy efficiency projects. To make up for this loss of expertise, agency officials reported taking steps such as having staff attend training courses to learn about a variety of energy topics, including alternative financing contracts.

Because the change to an energy-intensity-based metric does not always accurately reflect greenhouse gas emissions, we are recommending that the Secretary of Energy, in conjunction with the Federal Environmental Executive and the Director of the Office of Management and Budget, reevaluate the current measure for greenhouse gas emissions and establish one that more accurately reflects agencies' performance in reducing these emissions. We also are recommending that the Secretary of Energy finalize and issue guidance for agencies' use in developing long-term plans that contains key elements for meeting current and future energy goals.

In commenting on a draft of this chapter, NASA and USPS generally agreed with our findings, conclusions, and recommendations and provided written comments included as appendixes II and III, respectively. GSA responded by e-mail on September 8, 2008, stating that it concurred with our report. VA neither agreed nor disagreed with our report and provided written comments included as appendix IV. The Council on Environmental Quality, DOD, DOE, and OMB did not provide any comments on our draft. For those agencies who submitted technical and clarifying comments, we incorporated those as appropriate.

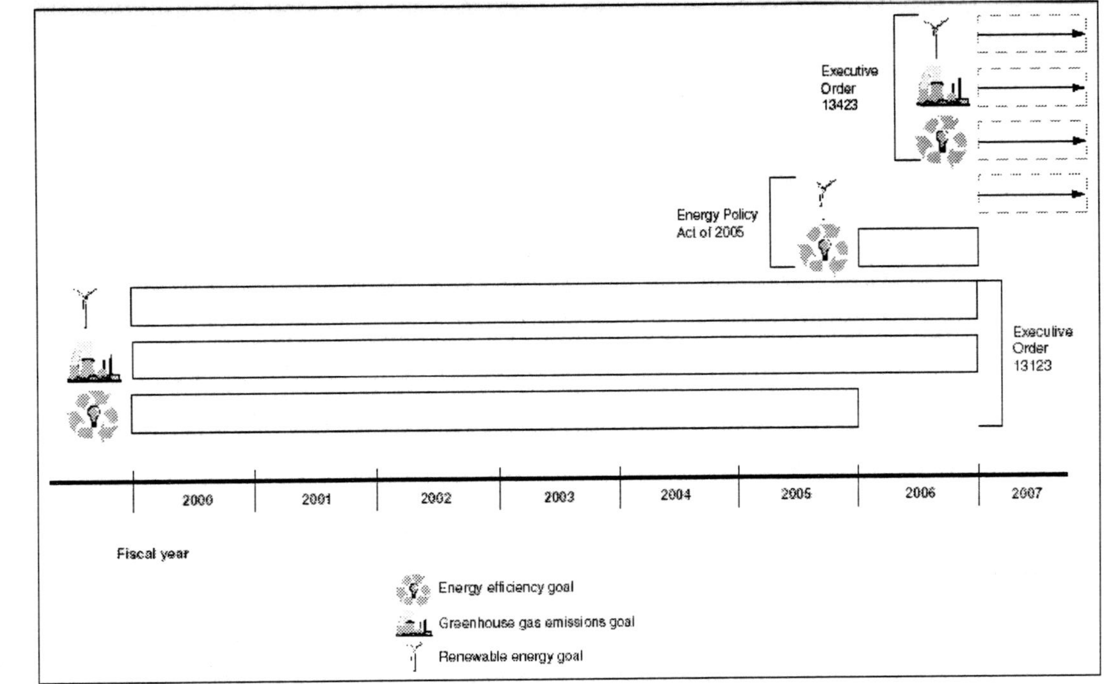

Sources: GAO analysis of EPAct 2005 and EOs 13123 and 13423 addressing federal energy conservation and uses; Art Explosion (clip art).

Note: The figure displays the energy goals that the agencies were to meet for a particular fiscal year. The dotted lines represent goals that are currently still in effect.

Figure 2. Timeline of Statute and Executive Orders with Energy Goals, Fiscal Years 2000–2007

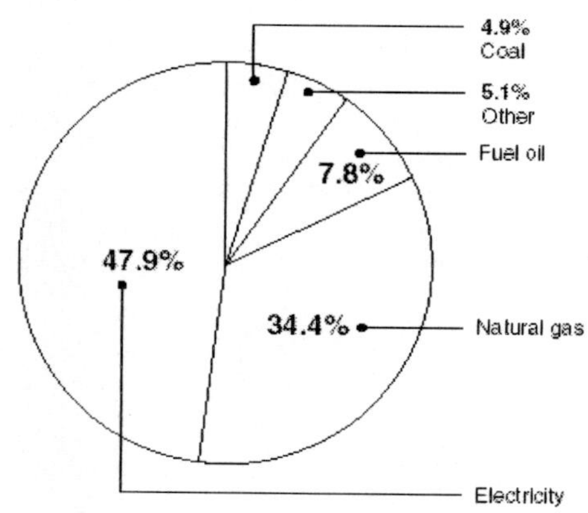

Source: DOE draft data.

Notes: This information is for federal buildings subject to the energy goals in EPAct 2005 and E.O. 13423 and does not factor in renewable or source energy credits agencies received.

Figure 3. Energy Consumed in Federal Buildings by Energy Type, Fiscal Year 2007

BACKGROUND

From fiscal year 2000 to fiscal year 2007, agencies were to meet the energy goals established by two executive orders and a statute as shown in figure 2.

Using energy data that agencies submit, DOE reports to Congress on agencies' performance toward meeting these energy goals. According to DOE, for fiscal year 2007, the buildings subject to these energy goals consumed approximately one-third of the energy consumed by the federal government as a whole.11 Federal buildings obtain this energy from a number of different energy types, as shown in figure 3.

According to 2007 national data from DOE's Energy Information Administration, electricity generation consists of coal (49 percent), natural gas (21 percent), nuclear electric power (19 percent), hydroelectric power (6 percent), and other (5 percent).

Carbon dioxide and certain other gases trap some of the sun's heat in the earth's atmosphere and prevent it from returning to space. The trapped heat warms the earth's climate, much like the process that occurs in a greenhouse. Hence, the gases that cause this effect are often referred to as greenhouse gases. Fuel types vary in the amount of greenhouse gases that they emit. For example, the burning of coal and oil emits greater quantities of greenhouse gases during energy use than other fossil fuels, such as natural gas. Renewable energy is produced from sources that cannot be depleted and, unlike fossil fuels, most renewable sources do not directly emit greenhouse gases.

DOE Reports That Most Federal Agencies Met Fiscal Year 2007 Energy Goals

According to draft data agencies provide to DOE, most of the 22 federal agencies reporting in fiscal year 2007 met the energy efficiency, greenhouse gas emission, and renewable energy goals. Some agencies used credits to meet the goals and would not have met the goals through reductions in energy intensity alone. Figure 4 shows the energy consumed, measured at the site where it is consumed rather than the source of the energy, in buildings that are subject to the energy goals, for 10 agencies with the highest energy consumption, in addition to the other 12 agencies reporting to DOE in fiscal year 2007. The other 12 agencies consumed a combined total of only about 4 percent of total site-delivered energy.

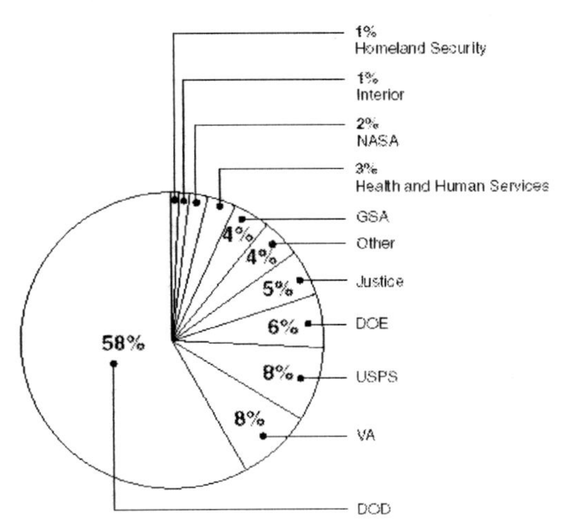

Source: DOE draft data.

Figure 4. Site Energy Consumed in Buildings Not Excluded from Energy Goals, Fiscal Year 2007

Energy efficiency. As figure 5 shows, all but one agency met the 2007 energy efficiency goal laid out in E.O. 13423, which calls for a 6 percent reduction in energy intensity from a 2003 baseline. Among the agencies held to the goal, only the Railroad Retirement Board missed it, reducing energy intensity by 5.8 percent from its 2003 baseline. The Environmental Protection Agency (EPA) reduced energy intensity by 63.8 percent from a 2003 baseline, which was the largest reduction among the agencies. As a whole, the 22 agencies met the energy efficiency goal, with agencies cumulatively reducing energy intensity by 11 percent from 2003 levels.

Use of credits for the purchase of renewable energy and source energy was common among agencies in 2007. USPS was the only agency that did not use any credits. Of the 21 agencies that used credits, 3 that met the energy efficiency goal with the credits would not have met the goal without them. EPA achieved the greatest percentage of its energy intensity reduction using credits—81.2 percent of its overall reduction in energy intensity came from the use of credits—representing about 5 percent of the total credits the federal government used. In contrast, about a third of DOD's reduction in energy intensity came from credits, but this reduction accounted for over half of all the credits the federal government used because DOD is overwhelmingly the largest consumer of energy in the government. Almost one-third of the total reduction in energy intensity reported by agencies is attributable to the use of credits.

Most agencies—21 of 22—used renewable energy purchase credits in fiscal year 2007. Five agencies also used source energy credits. For all agencies, renewable energy purchase credits accounted for about two- thirds of all credits used. Both types of credits were established under E.O. 13123. Source credits were aimed at helping the federal government reduce total energy use at the source of generation. According to DOE, renewable energy purchase credits were established to support the renewable energy industry. Although the credits were established to support federal energy policies, they do not reflect actual decreases in energy intensity.

Greenhouse gas emissions. The same 21 of 22 agencies met the 2007 greenhouse gas emissions goal under E.O. 13423, which holds agencies to the same standard as the energy efficiency goal—a 6 percent reduction in energy intensity from a 2003 baseline. The same renewable energy purchase and source energy credits that count toward the energy efficiency goal also count toward the greenhouse gas emissions goal.

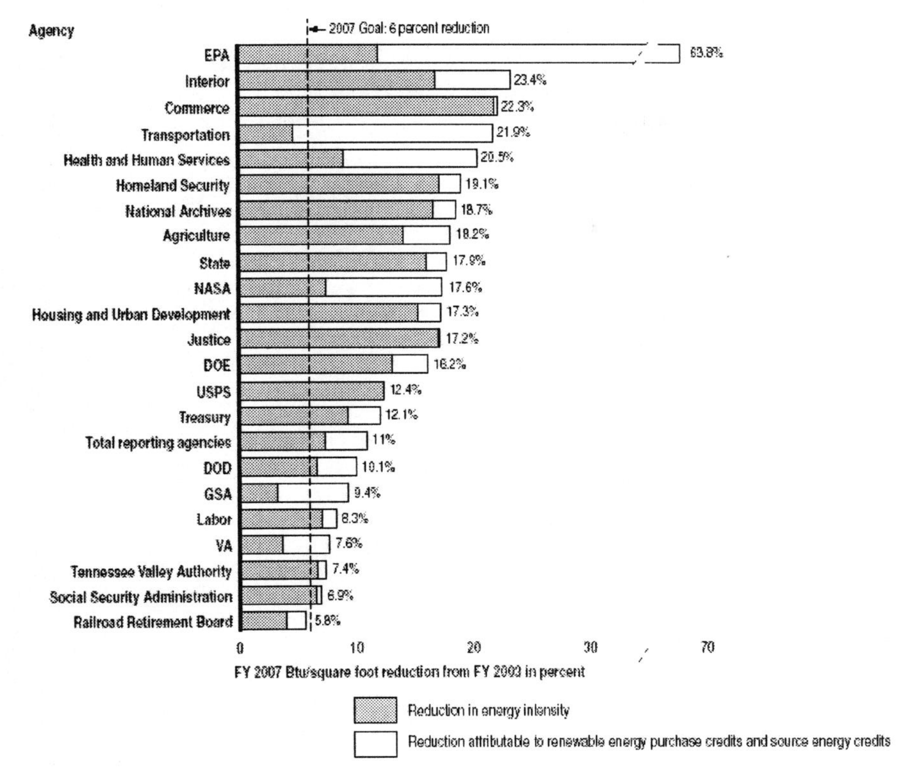

Source: DOE draft data.

Figure 5. Reduction in Energy Intensity from a Fiscal Year 2003 Baseline, Fiscal Year 2007

Renewable energy. Seventeen of the 22 agencies met the fiscal year 2007 renewable energy goal, as figure 6 shows. This goal requires that at least 3 percent of total electric energy consumption come from renewable energy sources, with at least half of the required renewable energy an agency consumes coming from resources put into service after January 1, 1999. The departments of Health and Human Services, Justice, and State; the Social Security Administration; and USPS missed the goal.[12] EPA achieved the greatest percentage of total electric consumption from renewable sources, with 153.5 percent. EPA was able to count more than 100 percent of its electricity consumption as renewable because it bought renewable energy certificates that exceeded the electricity it used, and because it received a small bonus for renewable energy generated on federal or Indian land.[13] As a whole, the federal government met the renewable energy goal, with 4.9 percent of its electricity use coming from renewable sources and at least half of this energy coming from newer renewable sources; only about 3 percent of the renewable energy total is attributable to bonuses.

ASSESSING PROGRESS TOWARD THE GOALS OVER TIME IS PROBLEMATIC DUE TO KEY CHANGES IN THE GOALS AND HOW PERFORMANCE IS MEASURED

Determining the extent to which agencies have made progress toward the goals over time is problematic due to key changes in the goals—as specified in statute and executive order—and how performance is measured. Performance can be compared across years when the way a goal is measured remains unchanged. After substantial change, however, there is no consistent measure against which to compare long-term progress toward the goals.

Energy efficiency. Key changes in the energy efficiency goal since 2005 illustrate the difficulty in making comparisons. As figure 7 shows, EPAct 2005 made key changes in both building categories and baseline years, and also changed the percentage reduction and the year by which agencies should have reduced energy intensity by that percentage.

These key changes make it problematic to compare agency performance against the goal before and after EPAct 2005 took effect. Although all but 1 of 22 agencies met the single energy efficiency goal in 2007 for buildings subject to the goal, according to draft DOE data, this performance cannot be directly compared with performance in 2005. In that year, only 8 of 17 agencies met the goal for standard buildings and 8 of 12 agencies met the goal for industrial and laboratory buildings.[14] Difficulty in comparing agency performance against the goal mainly resulted because of the key changes in building categories and baselines. The change from two building categories—standard and industrial and laboratory—to only one category changed the total square footage included in the energy intensity calculation.[15]

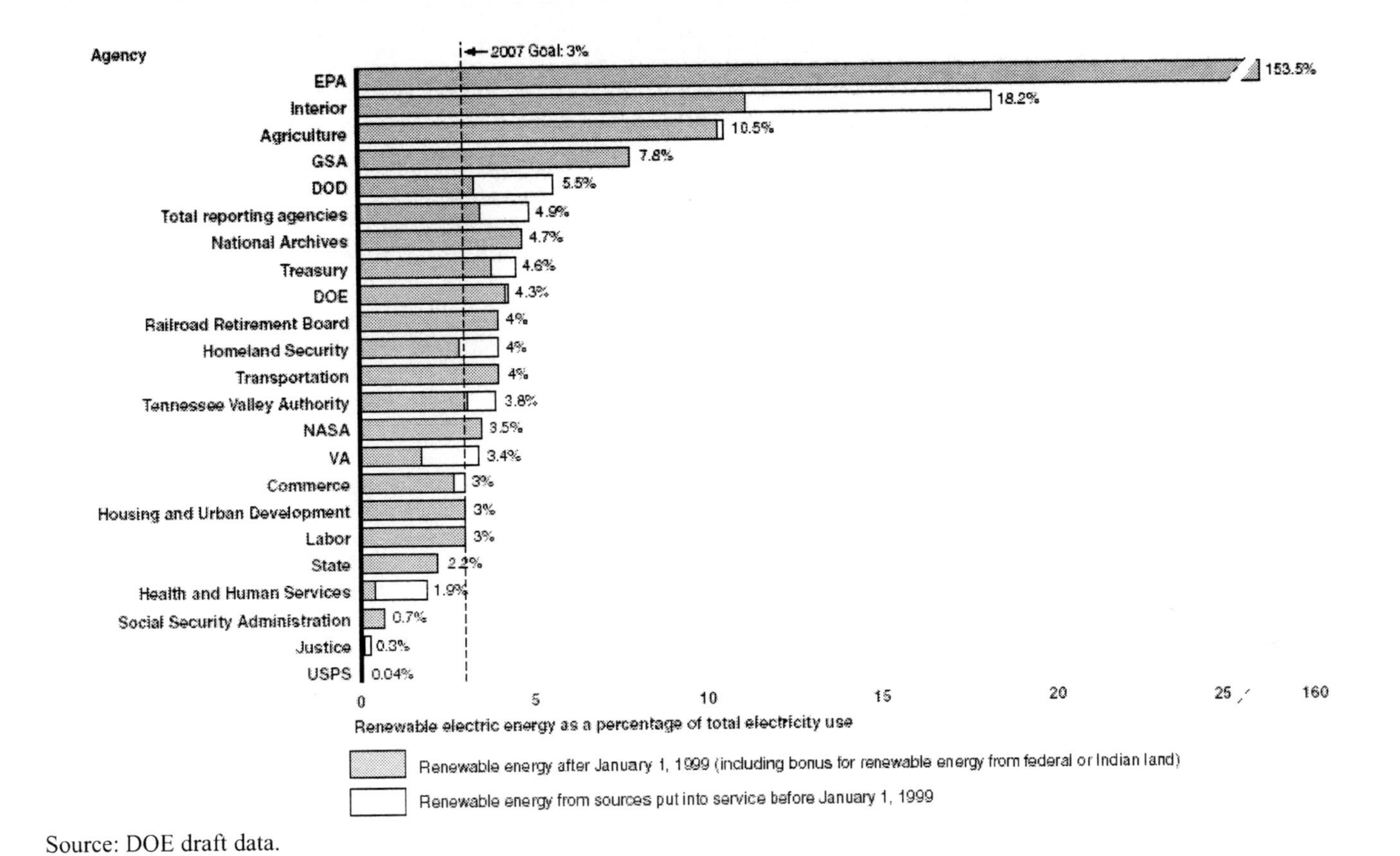

Source: DOE draft data.

Figure 6. Renewable Electric Energy Use as a Percentage of Total Electricity Use, Fiscal Year 2007

	Building categories	Baseline fiscal year[a]	Energy intensity reduction percentage	Final fiscal year by which agencies must meet goal
E.O. 13123	Standard	1985	35	2010
	Industrial and laboratory	1990	25	2010
EPAct 2005	All buildings	2003	20	2015
E.O. 13423	All buildings	2003	30	2015

Sources: GAO analysis of EPAct 2005 and EOs 13123 and 13423; Art Explosion (clip art).

Note: Buildings meeting certain criteria—such as those with a national security function—may be excluded from meeting the energy goals.

[a] Progress is determined by comparing the most recent data with the data for the baseline year.

Figure 7. Changes in How the Energy Efficiency Goal Is Measured

Data on NASA's performance against the energy efficiency goal in 2005 and 2007 show the difficulty in gauging progress after a key change to a goal. In 2005, the agency met the standard building goal by reducing energy intensity for those buildings by 30.4 percent against a 1985 baseline, exceeding the goal of 30 percent. It missed the industrial and laboratory building goal, reducing energy intensity for those buildings by 16.1 percent against a 1990 baseline, short of the goal of 20 percent. In 2007, NASA exceeded the goal for all buildings subject to the goal by reducing energy intensity by 17.6 percent against a 2003 baseline, well over the goal of a 6 percent reduction. However, because of changes in the baseline year and building categories, NASA's performance against the goal in 2007 cannot be directly compared with its performance in 2005 or earlier.

While we focused on how changes to measurement of the energy efficiency goal make assessing progress toward meeting the goal problematic, DOE also maintains actual energy intensity data for reporting agencies dating back to 1985. According to the data, agencies decreased energy intensity in all their buildings from 1985 to 2007 by approximately 14.3 percent. However, these data do not reflect the evolution of the energy efficiency goal during that period. For example, buildings that are excluded under the executive orders and EPAct 2005 are included in these totals.

	Measure	Baseline fiscal year[a]	Reduction percentage	Final fiscal year by which agencies must meet goal
E.O. 13123	Greenhouse gas emissions	1990	30	2010
E.O. 13423	Energy intensity	2003	30	2015

Sources: GAO analysis of EOs 13123 and 13423; Art Explosion (clip art).

[a] Progress is determined by comparing the most recent data with the data for the baseline year.

Figure 8. Changes in How the Greenhouse Gas Emissions Goal Is Measured

Greenhouse gas emissions. Similar comparative difficulties show up in examining progress toward the goal of reducing greenhouse gas emissions. Before 2007, under E.O. 13123, the goal called for reducing the amount of emissions by 30 percent by 2010 compared to a 1990 baseline. E.O. 13423 significantly changed how the federal government measures progress toward this goal. Now, the greenhouse gas emissions direction is measured using energy intensity against a 2003 baseline. Figure 8 shows the details of these changes.

Performance against the greenhouse gas emissions goal may be compared from 2000 to 2006, when E.O. 13123 remained in place and the goal was measured in the same way. However, the key change in E.O. 13423 from greenhouse gas emissions to energy intensity means that it is problematic to compare agency performance in 2007—when all but 1 agency met the greenhouse gas emissions goal—with performance in 2005—when only 7 of 21 agencies were on track to meet the goal. For example, VA actually increased its greenhouse gas emissions in 2005 by 20.3 percent from its 1990 level, and was far from meeting the greenhouse gas emissions goal of a 30 percent reduction by 2010. In 2007, however, it met the emissions goal because it exceeded the energy efficiency goal.

E.O. 13423 states that agencies are to reduce greenhouse gas emissions by reducing energy intensity. However, a reduction in energy intensity does not track directly with lower greenhouse gas emissions for two reasons. First, if an agency's energy consumption increases but square footage increases at a greater rate, then energy intensity is reduced while greenhouse gas emissions will increase, assuming all else remains unchanged. Second, the level of greenhouse gas emissions depends on the type of fuel used to generate energy. However, energy intensity does not account for different fuel types. Rates of carbon intensity vary by energy type per Btu delivered, especially for electricity, depending on whether it is generated from a fossil fuel, nuclear, or renewable source. Consequently, if an agency's square footage and energy consumption remain constant but the agency switches to sources that emit more greenhouse gases, such as switching from natural gas to coal, its energy intensity remains constant while greenhouse gas emissions increase. Conversely, switching from fossil-generated electricity to renewable electricity virtually eliminates greenhouse gas emissions. Although E.O. 13423 changed the measure for greenhouse gas emissions, DOE still estimates and reports greenhouse gas emissions by considering the sources used to produce energy and agency energy consumption.

The imperfect relationship between energy intensity and greenhouse gas emissions shows up in DOE data: we found cases in which energy intensity decreased over time, but greenhouse gas emissions increased. According to draft DOE data, at the Department of Commerce, for example, from 2003 to 2007, energy intensity decreased by 22.3 percent while greenhouse gas emissions increased by 2.4 percent. Similarly, the National Archives and Records Administration's energy intensity decreased by 18.7 percent over the period but greenhouse gas emissions increased by 21.5 percent. Although the National Archives and Records Administration's and the Department of Commerce's greenhouse gas emissions increased while energy intensity decreased, mostly attributable to increases in square footage of their building inventories, for the government as a whole greenhouse gas emissions decreased by 9.4 percent from 2003 to 2007 while energy intensity decreased by 11 percent.

It is not clear why the administration changed from an absolute emissions measure to one tied to energy intensity. When we asked about using energy intensity as a proxy for greenhouse gases, an official with OFEE told us that it is the administration's policy not to tie greenhouse gas emissions to a specific measure. Rather, it is the administration's policy to encourage agencies to voluntarily partner with other groups to reduce emissions, and the administration believes emissions will decline without a quantifiable goal.

Although energy intensity is an imperfect measure of greenhouse gas emissions, there is no scientific consensus on the best measure. Some organizations, such as the Energy Information Administration, a statistical agency of DOE which provides data, forecasts, and analyses, and the World Resources Institute,[16] have used or proposed several alternatives for measuring greenhouse gas emissions. Such measures include reporting total emissions, as was the case for the previous greenhouse gas emissions goal under E.O.

13123, and using greenhouse gas intensity measures. Some greenhouse gas measures, like the current energy intensity measure based on square footage, attempt to account for expanding or shrinking production or mission. Other proposed measures have included calculating greenhouse gas intensity by dividing total greenhouse gas emissions by building square footage or by units of performance or output, such as million dollars of gross domestic product or economic output, kilowatt hour, customer, or dollar of revenue. DOE, in its annual reports to Congress, estimates emissions from energy use in buildings that are subject to the goal, and presents annual emissions in metric tons of carbon dioxide equivalent, and in terms of metric tons of carbon dioxide equivalent per gross square foot.

None of the measures is perfect. For example, one agency official noted that an absolute emissions goal—as was used to measure emissions prior to the current measure—does not account for the fact that an agency may change its energy consumption or square footage to support its expanded or contracted work resulting from a change in mission. However, this absolute emissions measure allowed agencies to more easily track progress in reducing their total emissions. Imperfect metrics also are an issue at the international level. For example, one measure currently used by the Energy Information Administration is "emissions intensity," measured in emissions in a given year divided by the economic output for that year, which accounts for changes in national output. As past GAO work has shown, a decrease in this intensity-based measure may result in increased greenhouse gas emissions.[17]

	Percent renewable use required	Final fiscal year by which agencies must meet goal	Age of source to be counted
E.O. 13123	2.5	2005	All electric energy must come from projects built after 1990
EPAct 2005	3	2007-2009	Sources may have been placed in service in any year
	5	2010-2012	
	7.5	2013-and beyond	
E.O. 13423	3	2007-2009	One half of required renewable energy must come from sources placed in service from 1999 or later
	5	2010-2012	
	7.5	2013-and beyond	

Sources: GAO analysis of EPAct 2005 and EOs 13123 and 13423; Art Explosion (clip art).

Figure 9. Changes in How the Renewable Energy Goal Is Measured

Renewable energy. Key changes in the renewable energy goal since 2005 also make comparisons over time problematic. While both EPAct 2005 and E.O. 13423 specified different ages of renewable sources counted toward meeting the energy goal, E.O. 13423 did not change the percentage required or time frames required of the agencies, as figure 9 shows. Further, forms of nonelectric renewable energy such as solar thermal, geothermal, and biomass gas do not count toward the EPAct 2005 goal. E.O. 13123 did count these forms of renewable energy toward its goal.

Performance against the renewable energy goal may be compared from 2000 to 2006, when the goal remained unchanged. But the change in the age requirement for renewable sources makes it problematic to compare performance in 2007 with previous years. For example, although 17 of 22 agencies met the goal in 2007 and 10 of 20 met the goal in 2005, comparing performance in these 2 years is problematic because, with the 2007 goal, half of renewable energy came from sources in service from 1999 or later, but there is no source age specification for the other half. However, with the 2005 goal, all of the renewable energy came from energy sources in service in 1990 or later. Also, thermal renewable energy used in 2005 was not eligible to be counted toward the 2007 goal.

Data on VA's performance illustrate the difficulty in making comparisons when the age requirement for renewable energy sources has changed. In 2005, VA exceeded the goal of having 2.5 percent of its electricity consumption from renewable sources put into service since January 1, 1990, with 2.9 percent of its electricity consumption from these sources. In 2007, VA exceeded the new 3 percent goal, with 3.4 percent of its electricity from renewable sources, 1.8 percent from new sources put into service since 1999, and 1.6 percent from older eligible sources. Although VA increased its total renewable energy use, it is not clear whether its use from sources put into service since January 1, 1990, has increased or decreased, thereby making comparisons across the goals problematic.

AGENCIES' PROSPECTS FOR MEETING ENERGY GOALS IN THE FUTURE DEPEND ON ADDRESSING FOUR CHALLENGES

The prospects for meeting the energy goals in the future for the agencies we reviewed depend largely on overcoming four key challenges.[18] First, long-term plans can help clarify priorities and help agency staff pursue shared goals, but the six agencies we reviewed had long-term plans for achieving energy goals that lacked several of the key elements that we have identified in our prior work that make such plans effective. Second, achieving long-term energy goals will require major initial capital investments, but it is difficult for such investments to compete with other budget priorities. To address this problem, federal officials increasingly rely on alternative financing mechanisms; while these mechanisms provide benefits, they also present challenges. Third, agencies we reviewed face challenges in obtaining sufficiently reliable data on energy consumption; however, most agencies have tools for ensuring data are reliable and have plans to more accurately capture energy data. Finally, sites may lack staff dedicated to energy management, and also may find it difficult to retain staff with sufficient energy expertise;[19] lack of expertise could make it difficult to undertake alternative financing projects. Federal officials are participating in energy-related training courses and undertaking initiatives to hire, support, and reward energy management personnel.

Agencies' Planning Documents We Reviewed Lack Key Elements Needed to Guide Achievement of Long-term Energy Goals

Long-term plans can help clarify organizational priorities and unify agency staff in the pursuit of shared goals. These plans also must be updated to reflect changing circumstances, and according to our previous work, plans should include a number of key elements, including (1) approaches or strategies for achieving long-term goals; (2) strategies that are linked to goals and provide a framework for aligning agency activities, processes, and resources to attain the goals of the plan; (3) identification of the resources needed; (4) strategies that properly reflect and address external factors; and (5) reliable performance data needed to set goals, evaluate results, and improve performance.[20] Long-term plans with these elements help an agency define what it seeks to accomplish, identify the strategies it will use to achieve results, and determine how well it succeeds in achieving results and objectives.

While none of the six agencies we reviewed could provide us with what we considered to be a comprehensive, long-term energy plan, agency officials did provide numerous planning documents, including budget documents, strategies for improving energy efficiency, energy program guidance, and agencywide energy policies for sites. For the purposes of our review, we considered any of these planning documents, if they discussed actions to be taken beyond 12 months, as long-term energy plans. However, we determined that the long-term energy plans for one or more of the six agencies lacked some of the following key elements for effective long-term energy planning:

- approaches or strategies for achieving long-term energy goals;
- strategies that linked energy goals and provide a framework for aligning agency activities, processes, and resources to attain the goals of the plan;
- identification of the required resources needed to achieve long-term energy goals;
- strategies that properly reflect and address external factors; and
- provisions for obtaining reliable performance data needed to set goals, evaluate results, and improve performance.

Moreover, four of the six agencies' long-term plans were not updated to reflect E.O. 13423, although two of these agencies noted that they are in the process of updating these plans. In addition, in April 2008, the USPS Inspector General's office reported on the value of long-term energy plans and determined that USPS does not have a long-term energy management plan, and that without one USPS cannot effectively maximize its energy conservation efforts. The USPS Inspector General recommended the Postal Service develop and publish a National Energy Management Plan. This plan is expected to be published in early fiscal year 2009.

While long-term planning generally is recognized as an important tool in achieving goals, federal agencies have not been required to have long-term plans for energy goals. To close this gap, DOE is drafting guidance for agencies to follow as they develop multiyear plans and long-term strategies for assessing the level of investment necessary to meet energy goals, their progress in meeting these goals, and the likelihood that they will achieve these goals by 2015. Our preliminary review of the draft guidance found that it appears to address all of the key elements we identified. According to DOE officials, this guidance will be published in final form upon completion of DOE internal review, as well as analysis and reconciliation with new planning requirements in the EISA 2007.

In the interim, the six agencies are addressing long-term energy planning deficiencies in two ways. First, in recent years officials in agencies' headquarters have used short-term plans to achieve energy goals in the near term. All of the agencies that reported to DOE were required to provide annual plans under E.O. 13123 that included guidance on energy requirements and strategies each agency is taking over the next year to meet these requirements. However, E.O. 13423 does not require agencies to provide these annual plans. Agencies also used other planning tools to achieve energy goals in the short term. For example, GSA sets annual regional targets and requires each region to submit plans on how it will achieve these targets.[21] Agencies also submit budgetary documents requesting funds for specific energy projects.

Officials at the sites we visited had used a number of short-term plans to achieve energy improvements, but did not know how they would meet long-term energy goals. In several cases, these officials stated, they are planning to meet future energy goals by completing individual projects in the near term. For example, officials at one GSA site reported that they typically plan energy projects on a year-to-year basis, depending on the available funds, and did not have a long-term energy plan. At one USPS site, officials said they have not yet documented a comprehensive, longterm plan highlighting the steps they have taken or intend to take to ensure they reach energy goals. In addition, officials at a DOE site stated that it is difficult to plan a long-term approach for achieving energy goals because the site's mission is constantly evolving. Moreover, most military installations we visited did not have a long-term plan to achieve energy savings into the future and were instead developing individual projects to improve the energy efficiency in existing structures.

Second, agencies are using energy audits as a way to identify potential energy savings and meet long-term goals. In the past, we have reported that energy audits are a key strategy for identifying and evaluating future energy projects,[22] and officials at all the agencies we spoke with reported undertaking energy audits as a tool to identify and plan future energy projects.

- Since 1998, NASA has conducted reviews at each of its centers every 3 years to assess their energy and water management programs. The review requires center staff to participate in a self-assessment by responding to a set list of questions, confer with headquarters officials during a week-long site visit, and discuss review findings including recommendations.
- USPS currently is conducting energy audits for 60 million square feet of its 310 million square feet of facility space, which will identify close to 2 trillion Btus of potential savings upon completion.
- In 2007, VA conducted energy and water audits covering six regions and a total of 64 sites, or a total of 20 percent of its sites. During 2008,

VA officials expect to audit 30 percent of its sites, which include 116 sites in seven regions.

- Energy audits are part of the Air Force's energy program and were undertaken to identify additional energy-related projects, and act as measures of how to reduce energy consumption.

While short-term planning and energy audits help guide agencies' efforts toward meeting their goals in the near term, they do not address how the agencies will meet the goals through 2015.

Constrained Budgets Limit Agencies' Ability to Undertake Energy Projects, and Agencies Are Turning to Alternative Financing

Meeting long-term energy goals will require major initial capital investment. According to DOE, to meet the energy goals under E.O. 13423, the federal government would have to invest approximately $1.1 billion annually (beginning in fiscal year 2008, based on fiscal year 2007 performance) through 2015 on energy-related projects. In addition, in June 2007, ASE reported that meeting federal energy goals will require an investment of approximately $11 billion from 2009 through 2015, or $1.5 billion annually.[23]

Paying for this investment up front with appropriated funds may be difficult for agencies because energy projects compete with other budget priorities. As figure 10 shows, from fiscal years 2000 through 2007, upfront funding ranged from approximately $121 million to $335 million annually—well below the $1.1 billion level of investment needed annually to meet future energy goals, according to DOE's estimate. Furthermore, according to draft DOE data for fiscal year 2007, federal agencies will face an estimated $5.3 billion gap in appropriated funding for energy investment from fiscal year 2008 through 2015.

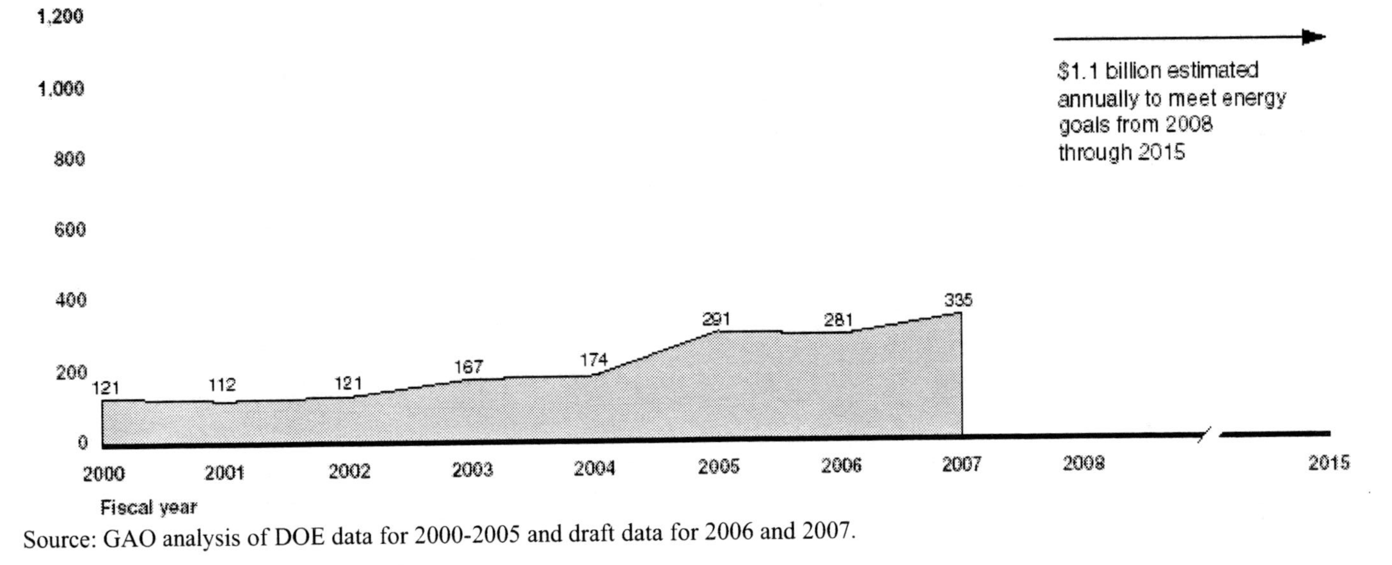

Source: GAO analysis of DOE data for 2000-2005 and draft data for 2006 and 2007.

Figure 10. Approximate Upfront Funding for Energy Projects, Fiscal Years 2000–2007

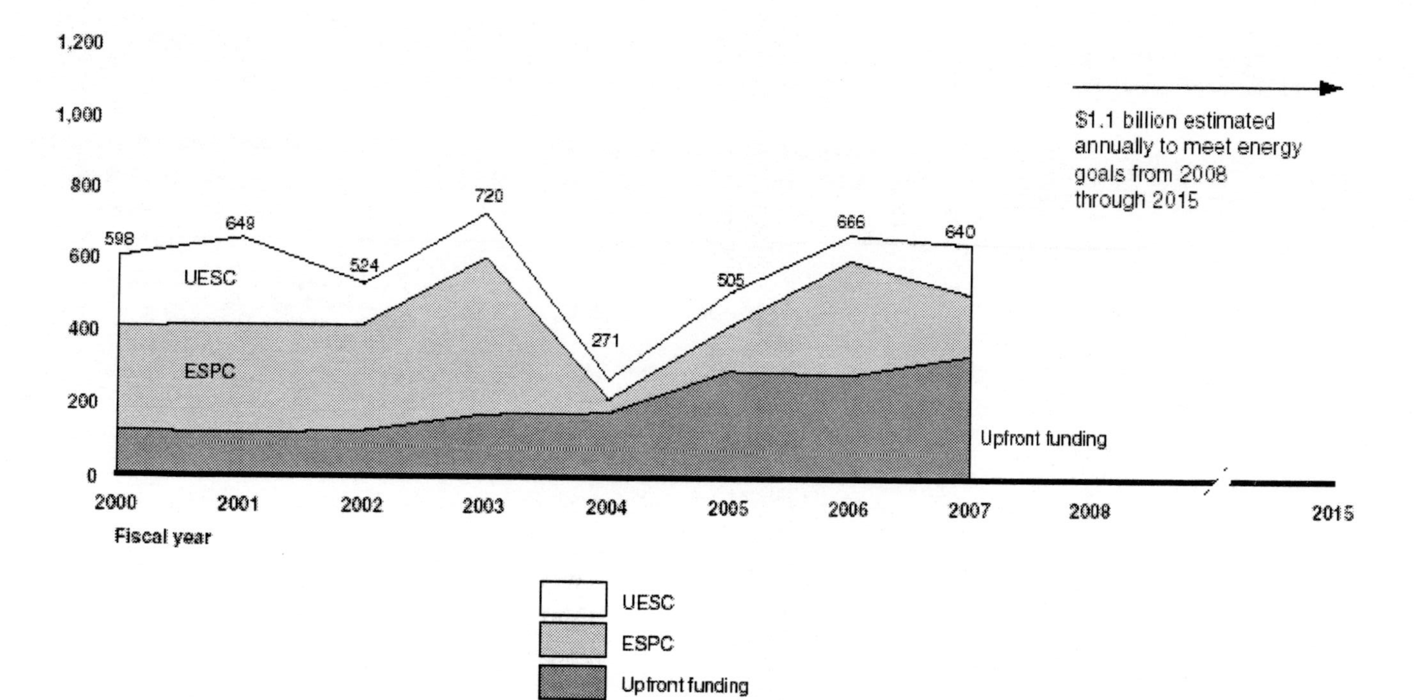

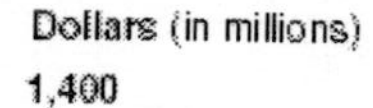

sources, such as operating and maintenance funding. ESPC authority lapsed on October 1, 2003, and was reinstated in October 2004.

Figure 11. Total Funding for Energy Projects by Funding Mechanism, Fiscal Years 2000–2007

Officials from all six agencies we reviewed cited budget constraints as a challenge to meeting future energy goals. For example, only 4 of the 10 military installations we visited have received upfront funding from DOD's Energy Conservation Investment Program since 2003.[24] Furthermore, several DOD installation officials told us that they no longer request funding for energy improvements because they do not believe upfront funding will be made available. In our previous work we similarly noted that agency officials had stopped requesting such funding. We also noted that paying for energy efficiency improvements with upfront funding is generally the most cost-effective means of acquiring them.[25]

Because the total amount of upfront funding is limited, federal officials increasingly rely on alternative financing mechanisms—such as contracts with private companies that initially pay for energy improvements and then receive compensation from the agencies over time from the monetary savings they realize from these projects—to meet energy goals. Seven of the 11 civilian sites and 9 of the 10 military installations we visited have used, are currently using, or are planning to use alternative financing to implement energy projects. Furthermore, in an August 2007 memo, the White House Council on Environmental Quality directed agency heads to enter into energy savings performance contracts (ESPC) and utility energy savings contracts (UESC) for at least 10 percent of annual energy costs to accomplish energy-related goals.[26] It further directed them to report on progress toward finding and developing alternatively financed projects.[27] Figure 11 shows the total amount of funding agencies received from upfront funding and alternative financing for UESCs and for ESPCs. As discussed earlier, most agencies met their fiscal year 2007 goals. However, for 2008 onward, if funding stays at the current level, there is an apparent gap between the amount received and the amount estimated to meet energy goals.

According to agency officials, alternative financing mechanisms offer benefits but also present challenges. In terms of benefits, these mechanisms can be used to complete energy projects and meet federal energy reduction goals when upfront funding is not available. For example, DOD officials stated that alternative financing mechanisms are necessary for DOD to meet future energy goals and, in March 2008 testimony before the Subcommittee on Readiness, House Committee on Armed Services, the Deputy Under Secretary of Defense for Installations and Environment stated that ESPCs typically account for more than half of all site energy savings.[28] Furthermore, according to DOD, the agency fell short of meeting past energy efficiency goals owing to a lapse in ESPC authority from October 2003 to October 2004. In addition,

DOE officials noted that alternative financing mechanisms provide large energy savings per dollar spent and estimated that ESPC project savings generally exceed guaranteed energy savings by about 10 percent. In 2005, we reported that agencies cited other benefits from alternatively financed projects, such as improved reliability of the newer equipment over the aging equipment it replaced, environmental improvements, and additional energy and financial savings once the contracts have been paid for.[29]

Agency officials also noted several challenges associated with such projects. For example, VA officials noted that development, execution, and ongoing administration of alternative financing contracts add overhead costs that increase the total cost of the contract. Furthermore, according to DOD officials, overseeing these contracts requires a level of expertise not always available at individual installations, and such contracts often take a long time to implement. In addition, officials at a number of civilian sites commented that developing alternatively financed projects requires a steep learning curve and the process for developing a contract can be time consuming. Finally, officials at a few agencies noted that in using these alternative financing mechanisms, it is difficult to measure and verify energy savings and to manage contracts with lengthy payback periods. Our June 2005 report also showed that agencies entering into these alternative finance contracts could not always verify whether energy savings were greater than project costs and may yield lower dollar savings than if timely, full, and upfront appropriations had been used. In addition, in our December 2004 report, DOD officials commented that the costs of using such contracts was 25 percent to 35 percent above what costs would have been in using upfront funds for certain energy projects.

Some agencies are undertaking initiatives to overcome the challenges associated with alternative financing.

- VA has created a central contracting center for energy projects, including alternatively financed projects. VA officials believe the center will offer a number of benefits, including the development of alternative financing expertise, increased accountability, greater agencywide awareness of these financing mechanisms, and standardization of the alternative financing process across VA.
- The Air Force, Army, and the Department of Navy have already centralized some functions in the process. The Air Force is working to further centralize these activities in order to decrease the number of staff needed to implement these contracts, and to review and approve all parts of the process in one location.

Furthermore, DOE's Federal Energy Management Program provides technical and design assistance to support the implementation of energy projects, including project facilitators who can guide site officials through the process of developing, awarding, and verifying savings from alternatively financed projects.

Agencies Face Measurement and Data Reliability Challenges but Are Taking Steps to Address Them

Collecting and reporting reliable energy data is critical for agencies to assess their progress toward their goals and identify opportunities for improvement. According to DOE officials responsible for overseeing the collection and reporting of energy information for the federal government, there are no federal energy measurement or data collection standards, and each agency gathers information differently, using its financial systems data and estimating data when necessary through other means. For example, NASA and USPS officials reported that their agencies use utility payment information to measure and report energy use.[30] Moreover, DOE officials stated that each site manager may use different means to measure and collect energy consumption, conservation, and cost data, including handwritten ledger sheets, software, cost averaging, and estimation techniques.

Measuring data at federal buildings is difficult if individual buildings do not have meters. Sometimes an entire site is metered by the local utility for usage and billing purposes, but not all of the buildings on the site are metered individually. Accordingly, energy managers cannot always reliably determine the usage in a specific building or group of buildings. Without meters, energy teams may be unable to pinpoint buildings or areas that need to be improved or identify which energy projects have effectively achieved energy savings.

In some instances, agencies' federal energy data have not been reliable. DOE officials responsible for annually reporting to Congress on agencies' progress toward energy goals acknowledge as much but stated that past year data are updated to correct inaccuracies discovered by the agencies.

- In April 2008, the USPS Office of Inspector General reported that USPS may be inaccurately reporting energy consumption data to DOE, and therefore cannot accurately determine its progress toward meeting the energy goals. Among other things, the Inspector General reported that USPS did not have a clear process for reporting data on sites' square footage and was calculating energy consumption by dividing billed cost by an estimated or average cost per kilowatt-hour, which can differ significantly from actual consumption.

- In 2006, a NASA energy management review reported that one of its sites had in some cases entered incomplete and erroneous data into the database the agency uses to track its progress toward energy goals.[31]
- A 2005 report from the VA Office of the Inspector General stated that the agency's energy data were not reliable because staff inaccurately reported sites' energy consumption and square footage. According to VA officials, VA implemented all of the recommendations in the report, including those addressing data reliability and, in September 2007, the VA Office of the Inspector General closed the report.
- Air Force officials stated that a thorough data review revealed data entry errors at approximately 5 percent of installations.

Agencies use a variety of mechanisms to verify energy data. For example, according to the DOE official who compiles agency data for the annual report to Congress, agency data reports are checked for any obvious problems by comparing the agency's energy information with their data from previous years to identify outliers. He also communicates with energy coordinators and compares unit price information with a site's recorded energy costs to determine if the reported costs appear reasonable. Beyond these checks, DOE relies on agencies' headquarters officials and the energy coordinators at sites to enter energy information for the sites and verify its accuracy. Many officials reported using quality control mechanisms to verify that current data match up with past records. These mechanisms include automatic database alerts, which notify officials of data that are outside specific ranges and thus could be errors.

Under EPAct 2005, agencies are required to install advanced electrical meters by 2012, whenever practical, to help ensure more reliable information. Advanced meters are capable of providing real-time data that feed directly into an agency's metering database, verifying savings from energy projects, and helping site officials to identify potential energy savings opportunities. According to the most recent OMB energy management scorecards, all six agencies we met with are meeting the milestones toward metering all appropriate sites by 2012.[32]

Some Sites Lack Expertise and Dedicated Energy Management Staff to Ensure Adherence to Goals, but Officials Are Taking Steps to Address These Challenges

To advance energy goals, it is important to have dedicated, knowledgeable, energy efficiency staff to plan and carry out energy projects. Moreover, according to a June 2007 ASE report, such staff can focus on identifying and implementing efficiency projects. However, some sites we visited did not have a full-time energy manager. Instead, staff members were often assigned part-time responsibility for performing energy-related duties in addition to duties unrelated to energy management, such as managing site maintenance and providing technical support and mechanical design assistance for a site. For example, at one DOE site, six to seven different officials have part-time energy management responsibilities. At other sites, a GSA building manager stated that he spends approximately 15 percent to 20 percent of his time on energy goals, and a NASA energy manager reported devoting approximately one-third of his time. Finally, officials at a Navy installation reported that there is no on-site, dedicated energy manager and that the installation needs one if it intends to meet the energy goals. In visiting military installations, we found that full-time energy managers tended to engage in multiple energy reduction activities, while other installations without full-time or experienced energy managers tended not to have robust energy reduction programs.

Furthermore, lack of expertise in energy management and high staff turnover may create challenges for negotiating and overseeing alternative financing mechanisms. Energy projects funded through alternative financing often require a high level of expertise in complex areas such as procurement, energy efficiency technology, and federal contracting rules. Many agencies told us that without experienced personnel, they face challenges in undertaking contracts that are necessary to meet energy goals. Officials from multiple agencies commented that high turnover rates exacerbate the difficulties associated with alternative financing.

To address these challenges, VA officials stated that they recently hired almost 90 permanent facility-level energy managers who will cover all VA facilities and focus solely on energy issues. DOD officials also reported using resource efficiency managers—contractors that work on-site at federal facilities to meet resource efficiency objectives with the goal of meeting or exceeding their salaries in energy savings. In addition, federal officials are taking part in energy-related training courses and undertaking initiatives to reward and support energy management personnel. Many agencies reported receiving training on ways to improve energy efficiency from a variety of sources, including agency-offered internal training, training provided by DOE's Federal Energy Management Program, and energy conferences. From fiscal years 2002 to 2006, agencies reported spending approximately $12.5 million to train more than 27,000 personnel in energy efficiency, renewable energy, and water conservation. In addition to training, the Federal Energy Management Program also recognizes outstanding accomplishments in energy efficiency and water conservation in the federal sector through an annual awards program. Furthermore, the White House annually honors federal agency energy management teams through the Presidential Awards for Leadership in Energy Management. Since 2000, these awards have recognized such teams for their efforts to promote and improve federal energy management and conservation and demonstrate leadership.

Conclusions

The current metric for greenhouse gas emissions—one based on energy intensity—is not a satisfactory proxy for assessing agencies' progress toward reducing these emissions. There is no consensus on a best measure at present; however, there are alternative measures that may better track agencies' greenhouse gas emissions than the current measure based on energy intensity. Although the previous metric—one based on emissions—had limitations, it was more clearly linked to emissions and made it easier to assess progress toward reducing those emissions. The closer a metric is to approximating the level of emissions, the better agencies will be able to determine their progress in reducing greenhouse gas emissions. In addition, although the ability of agencies to use renewable energy purchase and source energy credits towards the goals may further certain federal energy policy objectives, it also may enable agencies to achieve compliance with the energy goals without actually changing agencies' on- site energy use.

Although most agencies were able to meet their energy goals for 2007, without a strong plan of action agencies may not be well positioned to continue to achieve energy goals over the long term, especially in light of budget constraints and the $1.1 billion that DOE has estimated that agencies will need each year to achieve future energy goals. Furthermore, they face challenges with having reliable data and retaining dedicated and experienced energy personnel and have not adequately planned how to address these challenges in the long term. Without guidance from DOE that clearly outlines the key elements for effective, long-term energy planning identified in this chapter that could address these challenges, agencies do not have the foundation they need to develop plans that will continually adapt to a changing energy environment. As a result, agencies are likely to find it increasingly difficult to ensure that they will meet energy goals in the future.

RECOMMENDATIONS FOR EXECUTIVE ACTION

We recommend that the Secretary of Energy take the following two actions.

- In conjunction with the Federal Environmental Executive and the Director of the Office of Management and Budget, re-evaluate the current measure for greenhouse gas emissions and establish one that more accurately reflects agencies' performance in reducing these emissions to help determine whether agencies are making progress over time.
- To help agencies address the challenges they face in meeting energy goals into the future, finalize and issue guidance that instructs agencies in developing long-term energy plans that consider the key elements of effective plans identified in this chapter.

Terrell G. Dorn
Director, Physical Infrastructure

APPENDIX I

Table 1. Agencies and Site Visits Included within Scope of Engagement

Agency and service, as applicable	Site visit and location
Department of Defense	
Air Force	Fairchild Air Force Base, Wash.
	McChord Air Force Base, Wash.
	Offutt Air Force Base, Neb.
Army	Fort Benning, Ga.
	Fort Lewis, Wash.
	Fort McPherson, Ga.
	Fort Stewart, Ga.
Department of Navy	Naval Submarine Base Bangor, Wash.
	Naval Submarine Base Kings Bay, Ga.
	Naval Submarine Base New London, Conn.
Department of Energy	Forrestal and Germantown Buildings, Washington, D.C., and Germantown, Md.
	Sandia National Laboratories, Albuquerque, N.Mex.
Department of Veterans Affairs	VA Long Beach Healthcare System, Long Beach, Calif.
	Perry Point VA Medical Center, Perry Point, Md.
General Services Administration	Lafayette Building, Washington, D.C.
	Department of Veterans Affairs Administration Building, Washington, D.C.
National Aeronautics and Space Administration	Dryden Flight Research Center, Calif.
	Goddard Space Flight Center, Greenbelt, Md.
	Langley Research Center, Hampton, Va.
U.S. Postal Service	Curseen-Morris Processing and Distribution Center, Washington, D.C.
	Columbia Processing and Distribution Center, Columbia, S.C.

Source: GAO.

To ensure that we had a variety of sites, we selected the sites on the basis of both high and low reductions in energy intensity from 2003 to 2006, geographic location, site size, and agency recommendation, among other criteria. The six agencies and the sites we visited are listed in table 1.

We obtained and analyzed documentation and met with headquarters officials and officials responsible for energy management at the sites from the six agencies. In addition, we systematically reviewed these interviews to determine what primary challenges agencies face and the tools they use to meet energy goals. We used general modifiers (i.e., most, several, some, and a few) to characterize the extent to which agencies were facing and addressing the challenges we found. We used the following method to assign these modifiers to our statements: "most" and "many" represents four to five agencies, "several" and "some" represents three agencies, and "a few" represents two agencies. We also systematically reviewed documents and interviews to determine whether agencies' long-term plans contained key elements as identified by our past work.[33] For our review of agencies' long-term energy plans, we reviewed planning documents obtained from agency officials that laid out agencies' efforts to achieve the energy goals beyond 1 year. We also met with officials from the Alliance to Save Energy to get their perspective on challenges facing the federal government. Finally, we participated in DOE's Webcast training on energy savings performance contracts offered by DOE and attended GovEnergy, an energy training workshop and exposition for federal agencies.

We conducted this performance audit from May 2007 through September 2008 in accordance with generally accepted government auditing standards. Those standards require that we plan and perform the audit to obtain sufficient, appropriate evidence to provide a reasonable basis for our findings and conclusions based on our audit objectives. We believe that the evidence obtained provides a reasonable basis for our findings and conclusions based on our audit objectives.

APPENDIX II. COMMENTS FROM THE NATIONAL AERONAUTICS AND SPACE ADMINISTRATION

National Aeronautics and Space Administration
Headquarters
Washington, DC 20546-0001

September 11, 2008

Reply to Attn of: Office of Infrastructure and Administration

Mr. Mark Gaffigan
Director, Natural Resources Division
U.S. Government Accountability Office
441 G Street, NW
Washington, DC 20548

Mr. Terrell G. Dorn
Director, Physical Infrastructure
U.S. Government Accountability Office
441 G Street, NW
Washington, DC 20548

Dear Messrs. Gaffigan and Dorn:

The National Aeronautics and Space Administration (NASA) appreciates the opportunity to comment on your draft report entitled, Federal Energy Management: Addressing Challenges Through Better Plans and Clarifying the Greenhouse Gas Emissions Measure Will Help Meet Long-term Goals for Buildings (GAO-08-977).

Overall, NASA finds the draft report to be thorough, objective, and helpful in addressing one of our top Agency activities, energy management. We are pleased with your recognition of our positive steps and progress in this area, and we generally support the conclusion you have reached. If you have any question or require additional information, please contact Mr. James Leatherwood, Director of the Environmental Management Division, at 202-358-3608 or Mr. Wayne Thalasinos, NASA's Energy Manager, at 202-358-3811.

Sincerely,

Olga M. Dominguez
Assistant Administrator
Office of Infrastructure and Administration

APPENDIX III. COMMENTS FROM THE UNITED STATES POSTAL SERVICE

SAMUEL M. PULCRANO
VICE PRESIDENT, SUSTAINABILITY

UNITED STATES
POSTAL SERVICE

September 12, 2008

Mr. Mark Gaffigan
Director, Natural Resources and Environment
United States Government Accountability Office
441 G Street, NW
Washington, DC 20548-0001

Mr. Terry Dorn
Director, Physical Infrastructure Issues
441 G Street, NW
United States Government Accountability Office
Washington, DC 20548-0001

Dear Mr. Gaffigan and Mr. Dorn:

The U.S. Postal Service would like to take this opportunity to formally comment on the findings in the draft report entitled, FEDERAL ENERGY MANAGEMENT: Addressing Challenges Through Better Plans and Clarifying the Greenhouse Gas Emissions Measure Will Help Meet Long-term Goals for Buildings (GAO-08-977).

We generally agree with the findings contained in the draft report about the Postal Service efforts to reduce energy consumption and increase renewable energy use, however, we need to re-emphasize our position on specific issues. The Postal Service is reducing its energy consumption by focusing on those opportunities that provide a strong return on investment (ROI). Our objective is to be as energy efficient as is life cycle cost effective for both new construction and our existing buildings. In regard to renewable energy, given the current economics associated with the technologies, energy conservation is quite often a far better investment of financial resources. We are continuing to install and evaluate renewable technologies and will implement in those applications that are most financially viable.

By focusing on energy conservation and those opportunities that provide a strong ROI, the Postal Service is on target to meet the federal energy reduction objectives in its portfolio of 34,000 buildings without the use of outside financing or the purchase of credits. In addition, a national energy management plan is being reviewed by Postal Service leadership, identifying goals and standards for energy reduction and consumption for facility energy management, fleet management, fuel use and energy consumption. This plan will be released in the next 30 days.

If you or your staff wishes to discuss any of these comments further, I am available at your convenience.

Sincerely,

Samuel M. Pulcrano

475 L'Enfant Plaza SW Room 10647
Washington DC 20260-4232
(202) 268-2067

www.usps.com

APPENDIX IV. COMMENTS FROM THE DEPARTMENT OF VETERANS AFFAIRS

THE DEPUTY SECRETARY OF VETERANS AFFAIRS
WASHINGTON

September 16, 2008

Mr. Mark Gaffigan
Director
Natural Resources and Environment
U. S. Government Accountability Office
441 G Street, NW
Washington, DC 20548

Dear Mr. Gaffigan:

The Department of Veterans Affairs has reviewed your draft report, ***FEDERAL ENERGY MANAGEMENT: Addressing Challenges Through Better Plans and Clarifying the Greenhouse Gas Emissions Measure Will Help Meet Long-term Goals for Buildings*** (GAO-08-977). While we appreciate the opportunity to comment on the draft report, we were surprised that the Department was not afforded the opportunity of an exit conference with GAO.

Although the recommendations were not directed to the Secretary of Veterans Affairs, we have provided comments in the enclosure.

Sincerely yours,

Gordon H. Mansfield

End Notes

[1] Carbon dioxide is overwhelmingly the largest component of greenhouse gas emissions from energy use. Most carbon dioxide emissions in the United States result from the combustion of fossil fuels, the source of most of the electricity consumed in the United States.

[2] Renewable energy is produced from sources that cannot be depleted; such energy includes solar, wind, biomass, and geothermal.

[3] For ease of presentation, we refer to the greenhouse gas emission direction as an energy goal.

[4] Using DOE-determined criteria, certain sites and equipment may be exempted or excluded from having to meet the energy efficiency goals.

[5] Congress passed the Energy Independence and Security Act of 2007 (Pub. L. No. 110-140) in December 2007, which expanded the energy efficiency goal of EPAct 2005 and ultimately matched the goal of E.O. 13423 through fiscal year 2015. However, it was silent on specific greenhouse gas emission and renewable energy goals for federal agencies. We did not include the new law in the scope of our study because the law was passed in fiscal year 2008, which is beyond the time frame covered in our report.

[6] According to the U.S. Postal Service, while the agency is subject to the energy efficiency goal as laid out in EPAct 2005, it is neither subject to the act's renewable energy goal, nor is it subject to the energy goals laid out in the executive orders. However, it tries to comply with the spirit and intent of the energy goals.

[7] Small on-site, renewable energy generation projects that do not incur fuel costs, are unmetered, and are located on the customer side of a site's energy meter energy conservation project are not included in the total Btu-per-gross-square-foot calculations used for energy efficiency goals.

[8] Our work focused on the energy components of these goals, not on cost components. Although agencies are directed to achieve these goals with cost-effective or economically sound measures, cost savings is not the objective of these goals.

[9] GAO, *Agencies' Strategic Plans Under GPRA: Key Questions to Facilitate Congressional Review*, GAO/GGD-10.1.16 (Washington, D.C.: May 1997).

[10] GAO, *Energy Savings: Performance Contracts Offer Benefits, but Vigilance Is Needed to Protect Government Interests*, GAO-05-340 (Washington, D.C.: June 22, 2005).

[11] Vehicles/equipment and sites not subject to the statute and executive orders account for approximately 64 percent and 4 percent, respectively, of the energy used in fiscal year 2007.

[12] According to USPS, the agency is not subject to EPAct 2005's renewable energy goal. However, it tries to comply with the spirit and intent of the goal.

[13] Renewable energy can be purchased as renewable energy certificates (REC), which provide credit for the technological and environmental benefits of using electricity generated from renewable sources. A certificate can be sold separately from the underlying electricity with which it is associated. Once the REC is sold separately from the underlying electricity, the electricity is no longer considered renewable. Buyers of RECs can claim the credit for the renewable energy and may offset a percentage of their annual electricity use when green power products may not be available locally.

[14] Not all agencies have industrial and laboratory buildings.

[15] Agencies may apply to DOE for exclusion of certain buildings from the energy efficiency goal for a number of reasons, such as if a building is crucial to an agency's national security function. With the change from E.O. 13123 to EPAct 2005, the criteria for exclusions changed; as a result, the number of buildings meeting these new criteria and therefore eligible to be excluded also changed, resulting in corresponding changes to the buildings included in the energy intensity calculation.

[16] The World Resources Institute is an environmental think tank whose stated goal is to find practical ways to protect the earth and improve people's lives.

[17] GAO, *Climate Change: Trends in Greenhouse Gas Emissions and Emissions Intensity in the United States and Other High-Emitting Nations*, GAO-04-146R (Washington, D.C.: Oct. 28, 2003).

[18] While EISA 2007 is outside the scope of our engagement, it may help agencies address some of the challenges we identified. For example, the act requires agencies to have an energy manager responsible for overseeing energy efficiency criteria that covers, at a minimum, federal sites constituting at least 75 percent of site energy use at each agency.

[19] Sites may include more than one building.

[20] GAO, *Executive Guide: Effectively Implementing the Government Performance and Results Act,* GAO/GGD-96-118 (Washington, D.C.: June 1996); GAO/GGD-10.1.16.

[21] GSA is responsible for meeting the energy goals for those buildings for which it pays utilities.

[22] GAO, *Legislative Branch: Energy Audits Are Key to Strategy for Reducing Greenhouse Gas Emissions*, GAO-07-516 (Washington, D.C.: Apr. 25, 2007).

[23] Loper, Joe; Capanna, Steve; and Harris, Jeffrey, *Reducing Greenhouse Gas Emissions In Federal Buildings, Facilities and Vehicles,* Alliance to Save Energy (June 2007). The $1.5 billion annual figure is based on the average cost of savings for super Energy Savings Performance Contracts – contracts for which DOE has negotiated with energy services companies that have been prequalified via a competitive process – that the federal government has awarded since 1998. The figure assumes there is no inflation in cost per energy unit saved through 2015.

[24] The Energy Conservation Investment Program is a centrally managed, project-oriented, DOD-wide account which is programmed annually and represents the only direct DOD investment in conservation. The program is funded strictly through appropriations and requires congressional notification prior to project execution and periodic update of execution status.

[25] GAO, *Capital Financing: Partnerships and Energy Savings Performance Contracts Raise Budgeting and Monitoring Concerns*, GAO-05-55 (Washington, D.C.: Dec. 16, 2004).

[26] ESPCs differ from UESCs in that ESPCs are contracts with private energy savings companies whereas UESCs are contracts with a utility provider. While there are other alternative financing mechanisms available to agencies, ESPCs and UESCs are the primary mechanisms the agencies use.

[27] The Council on Environmental Quality coordinates federal environmental efforts and works with agencies and other White House offices in the development of environmental policies and initiatives. The Council reports annually to the President on the state of the environment, oversees federal agency implementation of the environmental impact assessment process, and acts as a referee when agencies disagree over the adequacy of such assessments. James L. Connaughton, Chairman, Council on Environmental Quality, *Substantially Increasing Federal Agency Use of Energy Savings Performance Contracting* (Aug. 3, 2007).

[28] Statement of Mr. Wayne Arny, Deputy Under Secretary of Defense (Installations and Environment), House Armed Services Committee, Readiness Subcommittee (Mar. 13, 2008).

[29] GAO, *Energy Savings: Performance Contracts Offer Benefits, but Vigilance Is Needed to Protect Government Interests*, GAO-05-340 (Washington, D.C.: June 22, 2005).

[30] USPS is in the process of developing and implementing two new systems that will allow officials to collect and track actual consumption data. According to USPS officials, the Enterprise Energy Management System will enable USPS to locally and remotely monitor energy usage and demand, as well as consolidate energy-related data from existing applications and facilities into a centralized location. The Utility Management System will uniformly collect actual utility energy cost and consumption data.

[31] NASA headquarters conducts reviews of each of its sites' energy management programs every 3 years.

[32] OMB reports progress toward creating a results-oriented government through scorecards, which are used to track how well departments and agencies are performing and where they stand at a given point in time against the overall standards for success.

[33] GAO, *Agencies' Strategic Plans Under GPRA: Key Questions to Facilitate Congressional Review*, GAO/GGD-10.1.16 (Washington, D.C.: May 1997).

INDEX

E

F

G

H

I

L

U

V

W